URBAN TRAILS
TACOMA

URBAN TRAILS

TRAILS
TACOMA

**Federal Way · Auburn
Puyallup · Anderson Island**

CRAIG ROMANO

MOUNTAINEERS
BOOKS

MOUNTAINEERS BOOKS is dedicated to the exploration, preservation, and enjoyment of outdoor and wilderness areas.

1001 SW Klickitat Way, Suite 201, Seattle, WA 98134
800-553-4453, www.mountaineersbooks.org

Printed in China
Distributed in the United Kingdom by Cordee, www.cordee.co.uk
First edition, 2019

Copyeditor: Erin Cusick
Design: Jen Grable
Layout: Kate Basart/Union Pageworks
Cartographer: Pease Press Cartography
All photographs by the author unless credited otherwise
Cover photograph: *Explore the heavily forested paths of Wildwood Park (Trail 40).*
Frontispiece: *Walk or run the peaceful Nathan Chapman Memorial Trail (Trail 43).*

Cataloging-in-Publication Data is on record at the Library of Congress.

Mountaineers Books titles may be purchased for corporate, educational, or other promotional sales, and our authors are available for a wide range of events. For information on special discounts or booking an author, contact our customer service at 800-553-4453 or mbooks@mountaineersbooks.org.

Printed on FSC®-certified materials

	MIX
FSC	Paper from responsible sources
www.fsc.org	FSC® C008047

ISBN (paperback): 978-1-68051-225-0
ISBN (ebook): 978-1-68051-226-7

An independent nonprofit publisher since 1960

CONTENTS

TACOMA

LAKEWOOD AREA

PUYALLUP

Trail Locator Map

TRAILS AT A GLANCE

Trail and/or Park	Distance	Walk	Hike	Run	Bike	Kids	Dogs
TACOMA							
1. Scott Pierson Trail (Tacoma Narrows Bridge)	3.4 miles roundtrip	•		•	•	•	•
2. Ruston Way and Waterwalk	3.2 miles one-way	•		•		•	•
3. Point Defiance Park	more than 15 miles of trails	•	•	•		•	•
4. Puget Creek Natural Area	1.8 miles roundtrip	•		•		•	•
5. Titlow Park	about 3 miles of trails	•		•		•	•
6. Chambers Creek Regional Park	more than 6 miles of trails	•		•	•		•
7. Tacoma Nature Center (Snake Lake)	about 2 miles of trails	•	•			•	
8. Wright Park	more than 2 miles of trails	•		•		•	•
9. Wapato Park	about 2 miles of trails	•		•			
10. Water Flume Line Trail	2.5 miles one-way	•		•	•	•	•
11. Swan Creek Park	more than 5 miles of trails	•	•	•	•	•	•
LAKEWOOD AREA							
12. Farrells Marsh Wildlife Area	about 1.5 miles of trails	•	•				•
13. Fort Steilacoom Park	more than 7 miles of trails	•	•	•	•	•	•
14. Spanaway Lake and Bresemann Forest	more than 5 miles of trails	•		•	•	•	•

Trail and/or Park	Distance	Walk	Hike	Run	Bike	Kids	Dogs
15. Sequalitchew Creek Trail	3.2 miles roundtrip		•	•		•	•
ANDERSON ISLAND							
16. Jane Cammon and Montalvo Parks	1.5 miles of trails	•	•	•	•	•	•
17. Andy's Marine Park	1.5 miles roundtrip		•			•	
18. Andy's Wildlife Park	2.1 miles of trails		•			•	•
19. Jacobs Point Park	2.5-mile loop		•			•	
FEDERAL WAY							
20. Dash Point State Park	more than 10 miles of trails	•	•	•	•	•	•
21. West Hylebos Wetlands Park	1.4 miles of trails	•	•			•	
22. BPA Trail	3.6 miles one-way	•		•	•	•	•
23. Milton Interurban Trail	2.5 miles one-way	•	•	•	•	•	•
AUBURN							
24. White River Trail	2.25 miles one-way	•		•	•		•
25. Interurban Trail	15 miles one-way	•		•	•	•	•
26. Green River College Trails	4 miles of trails	•	•	•		•	•
27. Green River Natural Area	more than 7 miles of trails	•	•	•	•	•	•
28. Flaming Geyser State Park	more than 5 miles of trails	•	•	•		•	•
MAPLE VALLEY, BLACK DIAMOND, AND ENUMCLAW							
29. Cedar River Trail	5.7 miles one-way	•	•	•	•	•	•
30. Green to Cedar Rivers Trail	3.3 miles one-way	•	•	•	•	•	•
31. Cedar Downs and Cedar Creek Parks	about 2.6 miles of trails	•	•	•	•	•	•

Trail and/or Park	Distance	Walk	Hike	Run	Bike	Kids	Dogs
32. Danville-Georgetown Open Space	more than 25 miles of trails	•	•	•		•	•
33. Black Diamond and Henry's Ridge Open Spaces	more than 15 miles of trails	•	•	•	•	•	•
34. Lake Sawyer Regional Park	2 miles roundtrip	•	•	•		•	•
35. Kanaskat-Palmer State Park	2.5 mile-loop		•			•	•
36. Nolte State Park	1.5 miles of trails	•	•	•	•	•	•
37. Pinnacle Peak	5 miles of trails		•			•	•
PUYALLUP							
38. Sumner Link Trail	5 miles one-way	•	•	•	•	•	•
39. Puyallup Riverwalk Trail	4 miles one-way	•	•	•	•	•	•
40. Wildwood Park	about 1.5 miles of trails	•		•		•	•
41. Bradley Lake Park	1.5 miles of trails	•		•		•	•
42. Puyallup Loop Trail (Clarks Creek Park)	more than 5 miles of trail	•	•	•		•	•
43. Nathan Chapman Memorial Trail	2.3 miles of trails	•		•	•	•	•
44. Foothills Trail	21 miles one-way	•		•	•	•	•

A pair of hikers rest near an old-growth giant in Point Defiance Park (Trail 3).

sites, and vibrant neighborhoods and communities. While we often equate hiking trails with the state's wildernesses and forests, there are plenty of areas of natural beauty and accessible trails in the midst of our population centers. The routes included here are designed to show you where you can go for a good run, long walk, or quick hike right in your own backyard.

This guide has two missions. One is to promote fitness and get you outside more often! A trip to Mount Rainier, North Cascades, or Olympic National Parks can be a major undertaking for many of us. But a quick outdoor getaway to a local park or trail can be done almost anytime—before work, during a lunch break, after work, or when we don't feel like fighting traffic and driving for miles. And all of these trails are available year-round, so you can walk, run, or hike every day by utilizing the trails within your own neighborhood. If you feel you are not getting outside enough or getting enough exercise, this book can help you achieve a healthier lifestyle.

Mission number two of this guide is to promote the local parks, preserves, and trails that exist within and near our urban areas. More than 4.8 million people (nearly a million in Pierce County alone) call the greater Puget Sound home. While conservationists continue to promote protection of our state's large roadless wild corners—and that is still important—it's equally important that we promote the preservation of natural areas and develop more trails and greenbelts right where people live. Why? For one thing, the Puget Sound area contains unique and threatened ecosystems that deserve to be protected as much as our wilder remote places. And we need to have usable and accessible trails where people live, work, and spend the majority of their time. Urban trails and parks allow folks to bond with nature and be outside on a regular basis. They help us cut our carbon footprint by giving us access to recreation without burning excessive gallons of fuel to reach a destination. They make it easier for us to commit to regular exercise programs, giving us safe and agreeable

Coyote along the Interurban Trail in Milton (Trail 23)

places to walk, run, and hike. And urban trails and parks also allow for disadvantaged populations—folks who may not have cars or the means to travel to one of our national parks or forests—a chance to experience nature and a healthy lifestyle too. As the greater Puget Sound area continues to grow in population and becomes increasingly more crowded and developed; it is all the more important that we support the expansion of our urban parks and trails.

So get out there, get fit, and have fun! And don't forget to advocate for more trails and parks.

Yellow rhododendron in Point Defiance's Rhododendron Garden (Trail 3)

HOW TO USE THIS GUIDE

THIS EASY-TO-USE GUIDE PROVIDES YOU with enough details to get out on the trail with confidence while leaving enough room for your own personal discovery. I have walked, hiked, or run every mile of the trails described here, and the directions and advice are accurate and up-to-date. Conditions can and do change, however, so make sure you check on the status of a park or trail before you go.

THE DESTINATIONS

This book includes forty-four destinations, covering trails in and around Tacoma, Lakewood, DuPont, Puyallup, Federal Way, Auburn, Sumner, Milton, Maple Valley, Black Diamond, Enumclaw, and Anderson Island. Each one begins with the park or trail name followed by a block of information detailing the following:

Distance. Here you will find roundtrip mileage (unless otherwise noted) if the route describes a single trail, or the total mileage of trails within the park, preserve, or greenway if the route gives an overview of the destination's trail system. Note that while I have measured most of the trails in this book with GPS and have consulted maps and governing land agencies, the distance stated may not always be exact—but it'll be pretty darn close.

Elevation gain. For individual trails, elevation gain is the *cumulative* difference on the route (and return), meaning not only the difference between the high and low points on the trail, but also for all other significant changes in elevation along the way. For destinations where multiple routes are given, as in a trail network within a park, the elevation gain applies to the trail with the most vertical rise on the route.

High point. The high point is the highest elevation of the trail or trail system described. Almost all of the trails in this book are at a relatively low elevation, ensuring mostly snow-free winter access.

Difficulty. This factor is based not only on length and elevation gain of a trail or trails, but also on the type of tread and surface area of the trail(s). Most of the trails in this book are easy or moderate for the average hiker, walker, or runner. Depending on your level of fitness, you may find the trails more or less difficult than described.

Fitness. This description denotes whether the trail is best for hikers, walkers, or runners. Generally, paved trails will be of more interest to walkers and runners, while rough, hilly trails will appeal more to hikers. Of course you are free to hike, walk, or run (unless running is specifically prohibited) on any of the trails in this book.

Family-friendly. Here you'll find notes on a trail's or park's suitability for children and any cautions to be aware of, such as cliffs, heavy mountain bike use, and so on. Some trails may be noted as suitable for jogger-strollers and wheelchairs.

Dog-friendly. This denotes whether dogs are allowed on the trail and what regulations (such as on leash and under control) apply.

Lush forest in Maple Valley's Lake Wilderness Park (Trail 30)

Tacoma's Chinese Reconciliation Park (Trail 2)

Amenities. The featured park's amenities can include privies, drinking water, benches, interpretive signs/displays, shelters, learning centers, and campgrounds, to name a few.

Contact/map. Here you'll find the name of the trail/and or park's managing agency where you can get current trail conditions. All websites and phone numbers for trail and park managers or governing agencies can be found in the Resources. These websites will often direct you to trail and park maps; in some cases, a better or supplemental map is noted (such as Green Trails).

GPS. GPS coordinates are provided for the main trailhead to help get you to the trail. Coordinates are based on the WGS84 data.

Before You Go. This section notes any fees or permits required, hours the park or preserve is open (if limited), closures, and any other special concerns.

Next, I describe how to get to the trailhead via your own vehicle or by public transport if available.

GETTING THERE. **Driving:** This section provides directions to the trailhead—generally from the nearest freeway exit in Tacoma or other population centers—and parking information. Often I state directions for more than one trailhead. **Transit:** If the trailhead is served by public transportation, this identifies the bus agency and line.

EACH TRAIL begins with an overview of the featured park and/or trail, highlighting its setting and character, with notes on the property's conservation history.

GET MOVING. This section describes the route or trails and what you might find on your hike, walk, or run, and may note additional highlights beyond the trail itself, such as points of historical or natural interest.

GO FARTHER. Here you'll find suggestions for making your hike, walk, or run longer within the featured park—or perhaps by combining this trip with an adjacent park or trail.

PERMITS, REGULATIONS, AND PARK FEES

Many of the trails and parks described in this book are managed by county and city parks departments, requiring no permits or fees. Destinations managed by Washington State Parks and the Washington Department of Natural Resources require a day-use fee in the form of the Discover Pass (www.discoverpass.wa.gov) for vehicle access. You can choose to purchase a day pass or an annual pass, and you can purchase the pass online, at many retail outlets, or from a state park office to avoid the handling fee. Each hike in this book clearly states if a fee is charged or a pass is required.

Regulations such as whether dogs are allowed or a park has restricted hours or is closed for certain occasions (such as during high fire danger or for wildlife management) are clearly spelled out in the trail information blocks.

ROAD AND TRAIL CONDITIONS

In general, trails change little year to year. But change can occur, and sometimes quickly. A heavy storm can wash out sections of a trail or an access road in moments. Windstorms can blow down multiple trees across trails, making paths impassable. Lack of adequate funding is also responsible for trail neglect and degradation. For some of the wilder destinations in this book, it is wise to contact the appropriate land manager after a significant weather event to check on current trail and road conditions.

Be appreciative of the thousands of volunteers who donate tens of thousands of hours to trail maintenance each year. The Washington Trails Association alone coordinates more than 150,000 hours of volunteer trail maintenance annually. But there is a need for more. Our trail system faces ever-increasing threats, including lack of adequate trail funding. Consider joining one or more of the trail and conservation groups listed in the Resources section.

OUTDOOR ETHICS

Strong, positive outdoor ethics include making sure you leave the trail (and park) in as good a condition as you found it—or even better. Get involved with groups and organizations that safeguard, watchdog, and advocate for land protection. And get on the phone and keyboard, and let land managers and public officials know how important protecting lands and trails is to you.

All of us who recreate in Washington's natural areas have a moral obligation and responsibility to respect and protect our natural heritage. Everything we do on the planet has an impact—and we should strive to have as little negative impact as possible. The Leave No Trace Center for Outdoor Ethics is

Champion red oak in Wright Park (Trail 8)

an educational, nonpartisan, nonprofit organization that was developed for responsible enjoyment and active stewardship of the outdoors. Their program helps educate outdoor enthusiasts about their recreational impacts and recommends techniques to prevent and minimize such impacts. While geared toward backcountry use, many Leave No Trace principles are also sound advice for urban and urban-fringe parks too, including these: plan ahead, dispose of waste properly, and be considerate of other visitors. Visit www.lnt.org to learn more.

TRAIL ETIQUETTE

We need to be sensitive not only to the environment surrounding our trails, but to other trail users as well. Some of the trails in this book are also open to mountain bikers and equestrians. When you encounter other trail users, whether they are hikers, runners, bicyclists, or horseback riders, the only hard-and-fast rule is to follow common sense and exercise simple courtesy. With this Golden Rule of Trail Etiquette firmly in mind, here are other things you can do during trail encounters to make everyone's trip more enjoyable:

- **Yield the right-of-way.** When meeting bicyclists or horseback riders, those of us on foot should move off the trail. This is because hikers, walkers, and runners are more mobile and flexible than other users, making it easier for us to quickly step off the trail.
- **Step aside for horses.** When meeting horseback riders specifically, step off the downhill side of the trail unless the terrain makes this difficult or dangerous. In that case, move to the uphill side of the trail, but crouch down a bit so you do not tower over the horses' heads. Also, make yourself visible so as not to spook the big beastie, and talk in a normal voice to the riders. This calms the horses. If walking with a dog, keep your buddy under control.
- **Stay on trails.** Don't cut switchbacks, take shortcuts, or make new trails; all lead to erosion and unsightly trail degradation.
- **Obey the rules specific to the trail or park you are visiting.** Many trails are closed to certain types of use, including dogs and mountain bikes. Some trails are bike only—don't walk on them.
- **Maintain control of dogs.** Trail users who bring dogs should have their dog on a leash or under very strict voice command at all times. And if leashes are required, then this *does* apply to you. Many trail users who have had negative encounters with dogs (actually with the

dog owners) on the trail are not fond of, or are even afraid of, encountering dogs. Respect their right *not* to be approached by your darling pooch. A well-behaved, leashed dog, however, can certainly help warm up these folks to a canine encounter.

- **Avoid disturbing wildlife.** Observe from a distance, resisting the urge to move closer to wildlife (use your telephoto lens instead). This not only keeps you safer but also prevents the animal from having to exert itself unnecessarily to flee from you.
- **Take only photographs.** Leave all natural features and historic artifacts as you found them for others to enjoy.
- **Never roll rocks off of trails or cliffs.** Gravity increases the impact of falling rocks exponentially, and you risk endangering lives below you.
- **Mind the music.** Not everyone (almost no one) wants to hear your blaring music. If you like listening to music while you run, hike, or walk, wear headphones and respect other trail users' right to peace and quiet—and to listening to nature's music.
- **Pack it in, pack it out.** Leave no trash behind. If hiking with a dog, remember that poop bags don't magically disappear. Pack them out and dispose of them properly.

HUNTING
Although nearly all of the destinations in this book are closed to hunting there are a couple of exceptions—they are noted in the route write-ups. While using trails in areas frequented seasonally by hunters, it is best to make yourself visible by donning an orange cap and vest. If hiking with a dog, your buddy should wear an orange vest too.

BEARS AND COUGARS
Washington harbors a healthy population of black bears in many of the parks and preserves along the urban fringe. If

you encounter a bear while hiking, you'll usually just catch a glimpse of its bear behind. But occasionally the bruin may actually want to get a look at *you*.

To avoid an un-*bear*-able encounter, practice bear-aware prudence: Always keep a safe distance. Remain calm, do not look a bear in the eyes, speak in a low tone, and do not run from it. Hold your arms out to appear as big as possible. Slowly move away. The bear may bluff-charge—do not run. Usually the bear will leave once it perceives it is not threatened. If it does attack, fight back using fists, rocks, trekking poles, or bear spray if you are carrying it.

Our state also supports a healthy population of *Felis concolor*. While cougar encounters are extremely rare, they do occur—even occasionally in parks and preserves on the urban fringe. In 2018 a bicyclist was killed by a cougar outside of North Bend. Cougars are cats—they're curious. They may follow hikers, but rarely attack adult humans. Minimize contact by not hiking or running alone and by avoiding carrion. If you do encounter a cougar, remember the big cat is looking for prey that can't or won't fight back. Do not run, as this may trigger its predator instinct. Stand up and face it. If you appear aggressive, the cougar will probably back down. Wave your arms, trekking poles, or a jacket over your head to appear bigger, and maintain eye contact. Pick up children and small dogs and back away slowly if you can do so safely, not taking your eyes off of it. If it attacks, throw things at it. Shout loudly. If it gets close, whack it with your trekking pole, fighting back aggressively.

WATER AND GEAR

While most of the trails in this book can be enjoyed without much preparation or gear, it is always a good idea to bring water, even if you're just out for a quick walk or run. Even better, carry a small pack with water, a few snacks, sunglasses, and a rain jacket.

THE TEN ESSENTIALS

If you are heading out for a longer adventure—perhaps an all-day hike in the Green River Natural Area—pack the Ten Essentials, items that are good to have on hand in an emergency:

1. **Navigation.** Carry a map of the area you plan to be in and know how to read it. A cell phone and GPS unit are good to have along too.

2. **Sun protection.** Even on wet days, carry sunscreen and sunglasses; you never know when the clouds will lift, and you can easily sunburn near water.

3. **Insulation.** Storms can and do blow in rapidly. Carry raingear, wind gear, and extra layers.

4. **Illumination.** If caught out after dark, you'll be glad you have a headlamp or flashlight so you can follow the trail home.

5. **First-aid supplies.** At the very least, your kit should include bandages, gauze, scissors, tape, tweezers, pain relievers, antiseptics, and perhaps a small first-aid manual.

6. **Fire.** While being forced to spend the night out is not likely on these trails, a campfire could provide welcome warmth in an emergency, with matches kept dry in a zip-lock bag.

7. **Repair kit and tools.** A pocketknife or multitool can come in handy, as can basic repair items such as nylon cord, safety pins, a small roll of duct tape, and a small tube of superglue.

8. **Nutrition.** Pack a handful of nuts or sports bars for emergency pick-me-ups.

9. **Hydration.** Bring enough water to keep you hydrated, and for longer treks, consider a means of water purification.

10. **Emergency shelter.** This can be as simple as a garbage bag or a rain poncho that can double as an emergency tarp.

TRAIL CONCERNS

By and large, our parks and trails are safe places. Common sense and vigilance, however, are still in order. This is true for all trail users, but particularly so for solo ones. Be aware of your surroundings at all times. Let someone know when and where you're headed out.

Sadly, car break-ins are a common occurrence at some of our parks and trailheads. Absolutely under no circumstances leave anything of value in your vehicle while out on the trail. Take your wallet and cell phone with you. A duffel bag on the back seat may contain dirty T-shirts, but a thief may think there's a laptop in it. Save yourself the hassle of returning to a busted window by not giving criminals a reason to clout your car.

Vagrants and substance abuse are concerns at several of our urban parks as well. It's best not to wander off trail, and if you come upon a homeless encampment, leave the area

MAP LEGEND

5	Interstate Highway	Campground/Campsite	
18	State Highway	View/Overlook	
	Surface Road	Summit	
	Minor Road	Building/Landmark	
	Unpaved Road	Bridge	
	Ferry	Gate	
	Hiking Route	River/Stream	
	Other Trail	Lake	
S	Start	Wetland/Marsh	
S	Alternative Start	Falls	
P	Parking	Park/Open Space	
	Restrooms/Privy	Other Parks	
	Picnic Area	Beach	
		Campus/Military Base	
		Railroad	

and report the situation to the authorities. Be aware of needles, human waste, and other hazardous debris around such encampments. I have omitted from this book any parks and trails where this is a serious concern.

No need to be paranoid, though, for our trails and parks are fairly safe places. Just use a little common sense and vigilance while you're out and about.

A NOTE ABOUT SAFETY

Safety is an important concern in all outdoor activities. No guidebook can alert you to every hazard or anticipate the limitations of every reader. Therefore, the descriptions of roads, trails, routes, and natural features in this book are not representations that a particular place or excursion will be safe for your party. When you follow any of the routes described in this book, you assume responsibility for your own safety. Under normal conditions, such excursions require the usual attention to traffic, road and trail conditions, weather, terrain, the capabilities of your party, and other factors. Because many of the lands in this book are subject to development or change of ownership, conditions may have changed since this book was written that make your use of some of these routes unwise. Always check for current conditions, obey posted private property signs, and avoid confrontations with property owners or managers. Keeping informed on current conditions and exercising common sense are the keys to a safe, enjoyable outing.

—Mountaineers Books

Next page: *Towering madronas and Douglas firs line the trail.*

TACOMA

With a population exceeding 210,000, Tacoma is Washington's third-largest city, and Puget Sound's "second city." Tacoma, the Pierce County seat, is situated on Commencement Bay, about halfway between Olympia and Seattle. It's one of the region's oldest cities and has long been the area's industrial powerhouse. Like Seattle, Tacoma's population exploded in the late 1800s with the arrival of the railroad. But the Emerald City would soon eclipse the City of Destiny in population, commerce, and regional influence.

Tacoma has gone through boom and bust periods, and its downtown core went into serious decline in the 1970s and 1980s. But an urban revival that began in the 1990s (and continues today) has brought revitalized neighborhoods, new museums, a University of Washington branch, and new life to the city, instilling a new pride. The city has long had a large military presence due to its proximity to the Joint Base Lewis-McChord. The city and neighboring communities have a diverse population, including the state's largest percentage of people of African descent. And recently the city has begun attracting young folks and families looking for more affordable housing and startup business opportunities than can be found in pricier nearby Seattle and the Eastside.

Tacoma has restored hundreds of historic properties, and many of its neighborhoods boast historic districts, giving the city a much older appearance than Seattle, where new developments have replaced many older structures and blocks. Tacoma sports a large park system and growing trail network. The city's Point Defiance Park is generally regarded by many, including this author, as one of the finest urban parks in America. And while large swaths of Tacoma contain drab industrial lands, the city has a stunning waterfront north of the port. On a clear day, from nearly everywhere in the city, you can see Mount Rainier (Tahoma), the city's namesake and pride, towering above it.

1

Scott Pierson Trail (Tacoma Narrows Bridge)

DISTANCE:	3.4 miles roundtrip
ELEVATION GAIN:	350 feet
HIGH POINT:	340 feet
DIFFICULTY:	Easy
FITNESS:	Walkers, runners, bikers
FAMILY-FRIENDLY:	Yes, and jogger-stroller friendly; beware of heavy bike use
DOG-FRIENDLY:	On leash
AMENITIES:	Benches, interpretive displays
CONTACT/MAP:	Pierce County Bike Map
GPS:	N 47 15.376, W 122 32.043
BEFORE YOU GO:	Check weather conditions, and avoid using during high winds

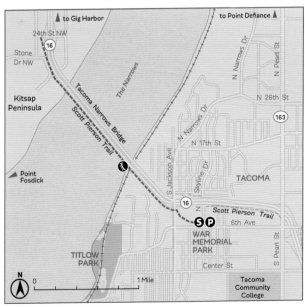

GETTING THERE

Driving: From Tacoma, follow State Route 16 north to exit 4. Then turn left onto N. Jackson Avenue and drive 0.3 mile. Next turn left onto 6th Avenue and proceed 0.2 mile, turning left into the Narrows Park and Ride. Continue left to reach the west end of the lot and the trailhead at War Memorial Park.

Transit: Pierce Transit line 100; Sound Transit line 595.

Walk or run across the fifth-longest suspension bridge in the country. The Scott Pierson Trail travels across the eastbound Tacoma Narrows Bridge, providing for pedestrians and cyclists a safe crossing of the impressive strait below. Noise can be intense from whizzing vehicles, and winds can be fierce across this Puget Sound passage. But the views of forested bluffs, Fox Island, and Mount Rainier are spectacular and provide a majestic backdrop to the bridges' massive steel towers.

GET MOVING

The paved Scott Pierson Trail travels for more than 6 miles from S. 25th Street near S. Sprague Avenue in Tacoma to 24th Street NW on the Kitsap Peninsula. Named for the urban planner who advocated for it, this trail parallels SR 16, offering a safe travel corridor for cyclists and pedestrians. The route is used heavily by cycling commuters, and most runners and walkers won't find much appeal to traveling along a busy noisy freeway. However, the stretch from War Memorial Park across the Tacoma Narrows Bridge is a thrilling and scenic walk or run.

Starting at War Memorial Park, follow the paved trail west down a grassy lawn lined with stately trees, memorials, and interpretive displays. The park was established in 1952 to honor the city's war dead. Within the park are also some displays on the Tacoma Narrows Bridge—which is actually a pair of high suspension bridges. A ferry from near Titlow Park (see Trail 5) once connected Tacoma to the Kitsap Peninsula. On July 1, 1940, the original Tacoma Narrows Bridge opened. But

Great view from the Tacoma Narrows Bridge

on November 7 of that year, during a windstorm, the structurally flawed bridge—the third longest in America—came crashing down. Nicknamed Galloping Gertie, the original Narrows Bridge's demise was viewed on film by millions, and the bridge forever became part of Northwest lore and history.

Ten years later a new bridge was opened and it still stands today. In 2007 a parallel bridge was built beside it to accommodate increased traffic. The two bridges, collectively known as the Tacoma Narrows Bridge, are the fifth-longest suspension bridges in America (behind New York's Verrazzano-Narrows and George Washington Bridges, California's Golden Gate Bridge and Michigan's Mackinac Bridge) and an impressive sight. Catch some good views of the bridges from the park. Then continue walking crossing N. Jackson Avenue and following the trail on a downhill slope to the bridges. You'll pass some old viewpoints with benches that have seen better days.

At about 0.7 mile, reach the bridges. The trail heads out onto the newer bridge servicing eastbound traffic. You are separated from the traffic by a solid concrete wall, but the traffic noise can be unnerving. Stay focused on the scenery.

Now start ascending—the bridge arches upward to a point nearly 200 feet above the strait below. If you have vertigo, you may want to consider a different trail.

Look west to the Kitsap Peninsula and a few Olympic peaks in the background. Look south along the Narrows to forested Titlow Park and Fox and Ketron Islands. And look back to Mount Rainier hovering on the eastern horizon. The bridge is more than a mile long, with two massive towers more than 500 feet tall that rise 300 feet above you. The cables supporting the structure are impressive, and you'll have time to marvel at them as you walk or run past them. Once you reach the Kitsap Peninsula, turn around and enjoy the bridge and views one more time.

GO FARTHER
You can continue north on the trail to 24th Street NW. Turn right and then left onto 14th Avenue NW and arrive, in 0.7 mile, at the 6.2-mile Cushman Trail.

2   Ruston Way and Waterwalk

DISTANCE:	3.2 miles one-way
ELEVATION GAIN:	Minimal
HIGH POINT:	10 feet
DIFFICULTY:	Easy
FITNESS:	Walkers, runners
FAMILY-FRIENDLY:	Yes, and jogger-stroller and wheelchair accessible
DOG-FRIENDLY:	On leash
AMENITIES:	Restrooms, benches, interpretive displays, historic sites, pocket beaches
CONTACT/MAP:	Metro Parks Tacoma
GPS:	N 47 16.519, W 122 27.678
BEFORE YOU GO:	Parks along the way are open from half hour before sunrise until half hour after sunset

GETTING THERE

Driving: From Tacoma, follow I-705 north to Schuster Parkway. Then continue north on Schuster Parkway for 1.4 miles. Bear left at the N. 30th Street exit and continue 0.4 mile on Ruston Way to street parking on your right. Additional parking areas are located along Ruston Way and on streets in Old Town.

Transit: Pierce Transit line 15 (a seasonal trolley) and line 13, which services McCarver Street, for access to the east end of the trail; Pierce Transit lines 10 and 11 servicing N. Pearl Street (State Route 163) for access to the west end of trail.

You'll be hard pressed to find a finer and more beautiful urban shoreline hike along Puget Sound than the Ruston Way Path and Waterwalk. Stroll or jog along Commencement Bay through a string of parks highlighting the natural, cultural, and

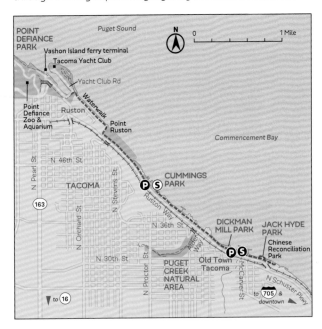

Ruston Way Path in Jack Hyde Park

human history of the area. Stare wide-eyed across sparkling waters to emerald Vashon Island, the jagged summits of the Olympic Mountains, and glacier-shrouded, massive Mount Rainier. And feel the pulse of Tacoma as you share these paths with a diverse array of folks.

GET MOVING

Any section of this 3.2-mile-long paved shoreline route will satisfy for a short walk. So if you're not intent on doing the whole thing, start where you may as there is parking nearly all along the way or nearby. Be forewarned, though, that on sunny days those parking spots fill fast. These two intercon-nected paths are also some of the city's most popular running spots. Running clubs and groups meet up here often. Con-sider joining them. And in between all the parks along the way, as well as gracing Tacoma's charming Old Town and modern Point Ruston, are scores of eateries, coffee shops, and brew pubs competing for your après walk or run celebrations and rejuvenations.

The Ruston Way Path's southeastern terminus begins in the fairly new Chinese Reconciliation Park. Wander through sobering memorials and interpretive displays highlighting one of Tacoma's and America's darkest and most disgraceful moments (see sidebar)—overt racism in the late nineteenth century against Chinese immigrants and Chinese Americans, which led to their expulsion from communities and exclusion from immigrating to the country.

CHINESE EXCLUSION

Sadly, Washington, like the rest of America, has an ugly racist past, particularly in the late 1800s, when waves of non-Anglo and non-Germanic immigrants were arriving in the country. Back East, Irish, Italian, Jewish, and other immigrant groups faced acts of overt racism. African Americans were subject to violence and Jim Crow laws in the South. And in the American West, indigenous peoples, people of Mexican heritage, and people of Chinese heritage were the targets of racist acts, laws, and policies.

Owing to competition for jobs, immigrants' willingness to work for lower wages, and straight-out racism, anti-Chinese sentiment in the 1880s was so strong in the United States that the US Congress passed (and President Arthur signed) two bills that prohibited the Chinese from further immigrating to America. It was the first time that laws were passed that specifically targeted a single ethnic group to stop them from immigrating to the country.

Tacoma went as far as expelling all its Chinese residents. There were more than one thousand Chinese laborers in Pierce County in 1885. Many were initially hired to work on the railroads, and afterward on the waterfront. In February of 1885, Tacoma's mayor, Jacob Weisbach (an immigrant from Germany), met with others to initiate ways to expel the city's Chinese population. The crowd adopted a resolution and later implemented policies to exclude Chinese people from Tacoma and to discourage others

After exploring this park, continue northwest through Jack Hyde Park, named for the former mayor who was responsible for the development of the Ruston Way waterfront. The trail hugs the shore, offering beautiful views north across the sound. The way then utilizes sidewalks and paths shaded by various hardwoods, passing by old piers and various restaurants and hotels. At 0.6 mile, reach Dickman Mill Park. Take time here to read about when Tacoma was referred to as America's Lumber Capital. The Dickman Lumber Mill operated here from the 1890s to 1974. It was the last of many mills that once bustled along this waterfront. Check out its ruins and the interpretive displays. Then keep walking northwest, passing pocket beaches and a slew of eateries.

from employing them. In September, an anti-Chinese council, presided over by the Tacoma mayor, met in Seattle, and proclaimed that all Chinese people must leave Western Washington by November 1.

Many Chinese soon left, but about two hundred remained in Tacoma. On November 3, a mob of nearly five hundred people, many armed with guns or clubs, marched through the city, stopping at each Chinese residence and business and telling them to pack and be ready for a wagon that would pick them up. No efforts were made by the governor or authorities to protect them.

Nearly two hundred Chinese were rounded up and forced to walk 8 miles in pouring rain to a train station, where they were forced to buy their own tickets to Portland. Those who couldn't afford tickets rode in boxcars or walked the 140 miles. Afterward, Tacoma residents burned down the city's Chinatown. No one tied to the expulsion was ever convicted, and several of the men involved became local heroes.

On November 30, 1993, the Tacoma City Council formally apologized for the Chinese expulsion of 1885. The council endorsed the construction of a Chinese commemorative park to be located at the former national guard site on Commencement Bay, close to the former Chinese settlement of Little Canton, from which residents were expelled. Walk through Chinese Reconciliation Park and reflect—in this age, can something this ugly happen again in this country?

At 1 mile, the trail comes to the junction of Alder Way and Ruston Way. You can walk left here 0.1 mile to the Puget Creek Natural Area (Trail 4) if you want a diversion. Otherwise keep strolling northwest, passing a beautifully restored historic fire boat. At 1.6 miles, pass through the manicured grounds of Cummings Park (alternative start). Enjoy good views here, too, from its piers. Lined with hardwoods (providing beautiful autumn colors), the way continues along the sound, arriving at the start of the Waterwalk at 2.5 miles.

Now follow the wide and new Waterwalk through Point Ruston, a newly redeveloped area of parks, high-rise condos, and busy retail shops and restaurants. Longtime residents will remember when this spot hosted a large copper smelter with its huge smokestack. The stack stood at 571-feet and was once the tallest stack in the world. The smelter closed in 1985, and the smokestack was imploded in 1993. The effects, however, of its toxic fallout continue to be felt throughout Tacoma, Vashon Island, and beyond, with health concerns and a multi-billion-dollar cleanup of contaminated soils.

Here, like the rest of the way you passed through, Tacoma's gritty industrial past has all but faded away, having been transformed into an inviting waterfront. At Point Ruston, the Waterwalk, along with a parallel gravel path, traverses well-tended lawns and crosses the Ruston city line (founded as a company town for the smelter) and ends near the Tacoma Yacht Club at 3.2 miles. The views west across Commencement Bay and east to Mount Rainier are among the best along the waterfront.

GO FARTHER

Walk a short distance left along Yacht Club Road and then follow a new paved path west for 0.5 mile to Point Defiance Park (Trail 3) with many more miles of trails awaiting your walking or running shoes.

3   **Point Defiance Park**

DISTANCE:	More than 15 miles of trails
ELEVATION GAIN:	Up to 350 feet
HIGH POINT:	300 feet
DIFFICULTY:	Easy
FITNESS:	Walkers, hikers, runners
FAMILY-FRIENDLY:	Yes, and some trails jogger-stroller friendly
DOG-FRIENDLY:	On leash
AMENITIES:	Benches, interpretive displays, water, restrooms, playground, picnic tables and shelters, zoo, botanical gardens, historic structures, beach
CONTACT/MAP:	Metro Parks Tacoma
GPS:	N 47 18.763, W 122 31.705
BEFORE YOU GO:	Open from half hour before sunrise until half hour after sunset

GETTING THERE

Driving: From Tacoma, follow State Route 16 north to exit 3. Then continue straight on Bantz Boulevard for 0.2 mile. Next turn right onto SR 163 (N. Pearl Street) and continue for 3 miles to a traffic circle. Exit traffic circle onto N. Waterfront Drive and enter Point Defiance Park. Follow this one-way road for 0.4 mile, continuing straight at overpass to Five Mile Drive. Then drive 0.5 mile on one-way Five Mile Drive, bearing right onto Owen Beach Road. Continue for 0.2 mile to large parking area and trailhead. Plenty of alternative parking lots and spaces are also available along Five Mile Drive.

Transit: Pierce Transit lines 10, 11, and 15 (a seasonal trolley).

One of America's finest urban parks, Point Defiance Park is the pride of Tacoma—and a Washington treasure. Walk, hike, or run on well-constructed trails through manicured gardens, along high coastal bluffs, and through spectacular groves of old-growth forest. Walk or run on a shoreline promenade, watching for seals or the early-morning or late-afternoon sunlight dancing on sparkling waters. And marvel at historic sites and some of the finest views of mountains, sound, and islands from any urban park anywhere.

GET MOVING

With more than 15 miles of trails traversing its 760 acres—and none of these paths open to bicycles—Point Defiance is truly a pedestrian paradise. Owen Beach, with its large parking lot,

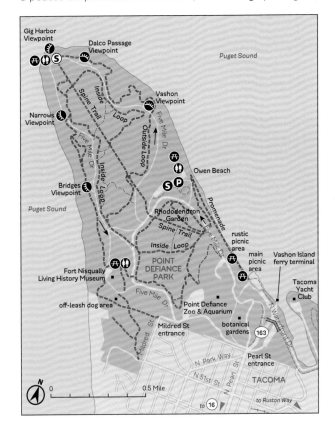

makes for a logical spot to head out on the park's trail system. But there are plenty of other parking places within the park and along Five Mile Drive if Owen is full or you wish to start elsewhere. And speaking of Five Mile Drive, popular with bikers, the outer loop of this scenic park drive is closed to vehicles Monday through Friday until 10:00 AM and on weekends until 1:00 PM, giving you even more miles of terrain to walk or run.

The park consists of three primary trails—the Outside Loop, Inside Loop, and Spine Trail—that form loops of varying distances, and a set of secondary trails that traverse the park and tie the primary trails together and allow for even more loops. The primary trails are wide, well groomed, and well signed. The park uses geometric shapes to label these trails on park signs and brochures and these are noted in the descriptions below. The primary trails make for some easy trail running and good hiking for folks of all ages and abilities.

The Outside Loop (Square Trail) pretty much travels the periphery of the Point Defiance peninsula on a 4.3-mile

Blooming rhododendrons in Point Defiance Park

journey. It travels to and through many of the park's scenic attractions. Pass several bluff-top viewpoints, revealing Vashon Island, Dalco Passage, Gig Harbor, and the Tacoma Narrows Bridge. The trail also passes by the Mountaineer Tree (named for the Tacoma branch of the Mountaineers); at 200 feet tall and 450 years old, it is one of the largest and oldest Douglas firs in the park. The Outside Loop passes through several picnic areas with restrooms. The trail also skirts the Fort Nisqually Living History Museum and the Point Defiance Zoo and Aquarium, two excellent family-friendly attractions that warrant all-day return visits.

The Outside Loop passes through the Rhododendron Garden too, which is absolutely stunning in bloom. Plan on visiting sometime in May. There is an additional half-mile loop trail through this natural garden. It will be a slow half mile as you will stand still, mesmerized at many of the multicolored blossoms. There are several dips along the Outside Loop and one little grind from the Rhododendron Garden back to the parking lot at Owen Beach.

The Inside Loop (Triangle Trail) travels 3.6 miles through the heart of the park's old-growth forest, staying away from the coastal bluffs and traveling primarily on more level ground. There is one good dip and a few minor ones along the way. Admire one of the finest urban old-growth forests: marvel at towering hemlocks, Douglas firs, and cedars in a thick understory of salal and evergreen huckleberries. Along the western stretches, pass by some fine madronas as well.

The Spine Trail (Circle Trail) traverses the park's peninsula in an almost linear fashion, from the Rhododendron Garden to the Gig Harbor Viewpoint. It's a 1.3-mile one-way journey with some ups and downs, including a 150-foot climb at the start.

And do consider checking out the paved 0.8-mile **Promenade**. You can access it from Owen Beach. This level path travels along Dalco Passage shoreline and through shady maple groves, delivering splendid maritime views. Vashon

Island is pretty prominent, and you can catch a glimpse of Mount Rainier. Look for seals and pelagic birds. And kids will like watching the ferries plying the passage.

Finally, if you are still looking for more paths to roam, head over to the park's eastern reaches and stroll through the botanical gardens. And if you want more, you can follow a new path over Pearl Street that delivers you to the Ruston Waterwalk (Trail 2) where you can keep going all the way to Old Town.

4 Puget Creek Natural Area

DISTANCE:	1.8 miles roundtrip
ELEVATION GAIN:	400 feet
HIGH POINT:	300 feet
DIFFICULTY:	Easy to moderate
FITNESS:	Walkers, runners
FAMILY-FRIENDLY:	Yes

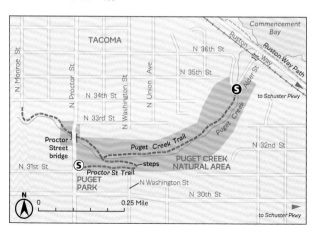

DOG-FRIENDLY:	On leash
AMENITIES:	Benches
CONTACT/MAP:	Metro Parks Tacoma
GPS:	N 47 16.519, W 122 27.678
BEFORE YOU GO:	Open from half hour before sunrise until half hour after sunset

GETTING THERE

Driving: From Tacoma, follow I-705 north to Schuster Parkway. Then continue north on Schuster Parkway for 1.4 miles. Bear left at the N. 30th Street exit and continue for 1.1 miles on Ruston Way. Then turn left onto Alder Street and proceed 0.1 mile to the trailhead on your left. Parking is limited. More parking is available along Ruston Way.

Transit: Pierce Transit line 15 (a seasonal trolley) stops along Ruston Way; Pierce Transit line 11 stops near the N. Proctor Street Trailhead.

Walk or run through a lush forested ravine beside a small salmon-spawning creek, one of the few remaining within the city limits. Wander beneath a beautiful and historic art deco bridge. Elevate your heart rate on a set of stairs climbing out of the ravine. And marvel at the remote atmosphere of this natural area located just minutes from the city's bustling waterfront.

GET MOVING

While the 66-acre Puget Creek Natural Area was established in the 1980s, adjacent Puget Park was created in the 1880s through a citizen donation. Several years later, gold was discovered within the creek, leading to a little bit of remorse from the original owner. However, the gold never amounted to much, thwarting any massive rush. Today the gold you'll strike here will be in the form of maple and cottonwood leaves in the autumn. The natural area is graced with quite a few deciduous trees, making for some nice leaf-kicking walks come September.

Maples and cottonwoods line the Proctor Street Trail.

From the Alder Way Trailhead, enter the natural area and begin walking on the Puget Creek Trail. It's a wide, smooth path lined with alders. Puget Creek tumbles alongside the trail. The path makes its way up a ravine cloaked in thick vegetation, revealing little that you are in a large city. The way steadily climbs, reaching a junction with the Proctor Street Trail just shy of a half mile. This trail heads left and, via a couple of switchbacks and a lot of steps, climbs 140 feet in 0.16 mile to little Puget Park on N. 31st and N. Proctor Streets. Definitely check it out, either now or on your return trip. With its accompanying split-rail fences, it's quite an attractive path.

The Puget Creek Trail continues up the ravine and travels under the beautiful 1927-built art deco Proctor Street bridge. The path eventually leaves the park (respect private property) and ends at 0.75 mile at N. Monroe Street. Now either retrace your steps or walk N. Monroe Street to 34th Street and then head right on Proctor Street over the bridge. Peer down the ravine and continue a little farther to take the Proctor Street Trail back into the ravine. This little street-walk connector is about 0.3 mile and allows you to make a nice figure-eight lollipop loop hike.

GO FARTHER
You can easily combine a walk or run here with the nearby Ruston Way Path (Trail 2).

5 Titlow Park

DISTANCE:	About 3 miles of trails
ELEVATION GAIN:	Up to 60 feet
HIGH POINT:	60 feet
DIFFICULTY:	Easy
FITNESS:	Walkers, runners
FAMILY-FRIENDLY:	Yes, and some trails jogger-stroller and wheelchair accessible
DOG-FRIENDLY:	On leash
AMENITIES:	Benches, interpretive displays, water, restrooms, water "sprayground," playground and picnic tables
CONTACT/MAP:	Metro Parks Tacoma
GPS:	N 47 14.883, W 122 32.990
BEFORE YOU GO:	Open from half hour before sunrise until half hour after sunset

GETTING THERE

Driving: From Tacoma, follow State Route 16 north to exit 4. Then turn left onto N. Jackson Avenue and drive 0.3 mile. Next turn right onto 6th Avenue and proceed 1.2 miles, turning right into the park and parking area.

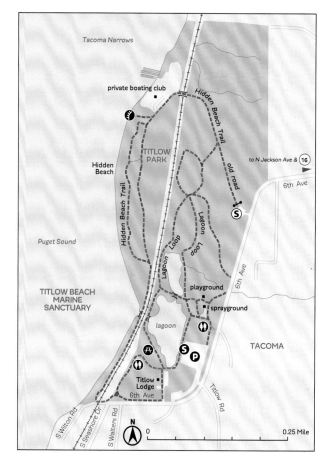

A hidden beach, a historic lodge, and splendid views of the Tacoma Narrows, Olympic Mountains, and Fox Island are what you can expect at this lovely park. Wander around a lagoon, through forests of madronas, and along Puget Sound shoreline. Watch for sundry birds and marine mammals, and witness some of the finest sunsets on the South Sound.

GET MOVING

What is now Titlow Park, a lovely 75-acre park along the Tacoma Narrows, started out as a resort. In 1911, Aaron Titlow set out to build the state's first tidewater hotel at this site—at the time a location far-removed from the city. Hiring a noted architect, he had a three-story Swiss-chalet-style lodge constructed, which he named the Hotel Hesperides. Food at the hotel was served from Titlow's 200-acre farm. After Titlow died in 1923, Metro Parks purchased the property and continued to operate the hotel.

The Great Depression, however, brought tough times to the hotel, and it was nearly demolished. The Works Progress Administration restored some of it in 1938—and the city renovated it in 2011. Today the Titlow Lodge is a beloved structure used for private gatherings, weddings, and other events. Wander around the grounds admiring the park's centerpiece—then take to the trails! There are about 3 miles of trails in the park, with two well-defined loops.

The shorter of the two is the 0.75-mile Lagoon Loop. Walk this trail along the shores of a saltwater lagoon. It is particularly interesting during low tide, often revealing a bevy of life. The lagoon consists of two separate pools. There's a short trail that utilizes a bridge crossing the small channel connecting the pools. The lagoon, along with much of the park, has recently been rehabilitated after years of degradation. East of the lagoons, find manicured lawns and a popular sprayground, where there was once an old saltwater pool.

Beach near old ferry landing

The longer loop is the Hidden Beach Trail. This 1.3-mile trail utilizes a short section of the Lagoon Loop and then continues to the north end of the park through a forest of alders and cascaras. It then follows an old road, crossing a set of railroad tracks on an old wooden bridge. From here it skirts a private boating club and then winds its way south along a wooded shoreline bluff graced with many fine madronas. Hidden Beach lies just to the west—and when the tide is low, you may opt to walk it instead of continuing on the trail. The views of the Tacoma Narrows Bridge are exceptionally good from the sandy beach.

The trail continues south and becomes paved, crossing the lagoon inlet and paralleling a set of railroad tracks. It passes more sandy beach and the site of the old ferry landing that once serviced Fox Island and Point Fosdick on the Kitsap Peninsula before the Tacoma Narrows Bridge was built in the early 1940s. Now carefully cross the active rail lines and return to the parking areas near the lodge.

6 Chambers Creek Regional Park

DISTANCE:	More than 6 miles of trails
ELEVATION GAIN:	Up to 230 feet
HIGH POINT:	230 feet
DIFFICULTY:	Easy
FITNESS:	Walkers, runners, bikers
FAMILY-FRIENDLY:	Yes, and some trails jogger-stroller and wheelchair accessible
DOG-FRIENDLY:	On-leash and off-leash areas
AMENITIES:	Benches, interpretive displays, water, restrooms, playground, picnic tables, beach, golf course
CONTACT/MAP:	Pierce County Parks and Recreation
GPS:	N 47 12.770, W 122 34.533
BEFORE YOU GO:	Open from half hour before sunrise until half hour after sunset

GETTING THERE

Driving: From Tacoma, follow I-5 south to exit 130. Then head right (west) on S. 56th Street and proceed for 2.4 miles to a traffic circle. Continue west on Cirque Drive W. for 2.7 miles to another traffic circle. Now head south on Grandview Drive W. for 0.8 mile and turn right onto the Chambers Creek Regional Park access road. Continue 0.5 mile to the large parking area and trailhead.

One of the most unique urban parks in the Northwest, the sprawling 930-acre Chambers Creek Regional Park encompasses a reclaimed gravel quarry—once the largest gravel- and sand-producing mine in the nation. Walk or run paved trails on the periphery of the old quarry—a greening moon-like landscape that now contains a world-class golf course. Savor spectacular island-dotted, peninsula-probing Salish Sea views. And explore nearly 2 miles of beach.

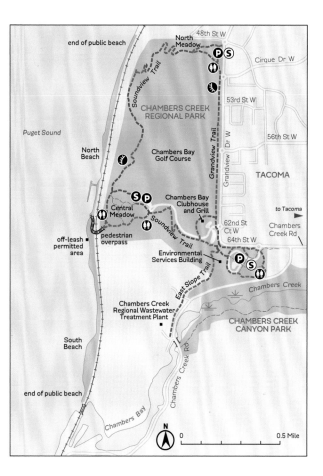

GET MOVING

One of the region's newer parks, Chambers Creek has a long and fascinating history. It was originally the site of a Steilacoom Indian fishing village, and the Hudson Bay Company established a trading post nearby in the 1830s. The area was then transformed from army post to timber mills and other

Soundview Trail travels through the Chambers Bay Golf Course.

industrial endeavors. In the 1890s, gravel mining began here and continued on a massive scale until 2003. After that, the county began reclaiming the mine by establishing a beautiful regional park and golf course. The Chambers Bay Golf Course received national attention in 2015 when it hosted the US Open.

Upon first glance, the park has an eerie beauty to it—looking like it belongs in the Scottish moorland or on the moon after a green revolution. More than one hundred years of intensive open-pit mining can radically alter a landscape. A whole lot of coastal bluff was removed and used for a whole lot of construction projects around the region.

From the main parking area, you can walk on some easy, short loop trails circling around the Central Meadow. Here too you'll find a spur trail leading to an overpass of the busy adjacent railroad tracks and delivering you to the beach (contaminated—no swimming). Plan for a low tide, and you have nearly 2 miles of public beach to walk. There's an off-leash area near where the trail meets the beach.

The classic loop at this park follows the Soundview and Grandview Trails. These two connected paved trails circle the park for a distance of 3.25 miles. From the main parking area, head north on the Soundview Trail (for a downhill finish) and pass by some of the ruins of the old quarry operation. They almost look like ancient Roman ruins, and you'll have fun photographing them. The trail then traverses the golf course, where signs warn of stray golf balls and their inherent risks.

While keeping an eye out for birdies and bogies, enjoy great views of the sound and of nearby Anderson, McNeil, and Fox Islands. The trail eventually enters forests and begins weaving upward, gaining more than 200 feet. The trail reaches the North Meadow, where the Grandview Trail now takes over. Pass a popular playground and parking area—a good place to begin if you just want to walk or run the Grandview Trail and skip all of the elevation gain and loss of the loop.

The Grandview Trail then heads south along the rim of the old quarry operation. It is nearly level, lined with madronas, and, as its name implies, provides grand views over the golf course out to the sound. The trail then passes the Chambers Bay Clubhouse and Grill, crosses the access road, and ends at a junction. Straight ahead are trails leading to the Environmental Services Building, parking areas, and ball fields. The Soundview Trail departs west (right) and begins a long descent back to your start to close the loop.

Other trails to consider are the short loops near the Environmental Services Building. There are some historical artifacts here, and some beautifully landscaped grounds with plenty of oaks and tulip poplar trees. The half-mile East Slope Trail departs from this area too, descending more than 150 feet to terminate near the wastewater treatment plant and the trailhead for the Chambers Creek Canyon Park (see Go Farther) across the Chambers Creek Road bridge. Head out and back on the East Slope Trail for a good workout and a generally quiet course. By combining all of the park's trails, you can get a serious run in or an all-day walk.

GO FARTHER

Nearby is Chambers Creek Canyon Park, which has a couple of short dirt trails totaling about 1.5 miles. Parking is difficult at the trailhead on busy Chambers Creek Road, and the trails are not connected (eastern access is from Kobayashi Park). The county, in cooperation with the cities of University Place and Lakewood, will soon be upgrading the park's parking area and expanding and connecting the trails, all sure to make this area a draw.

7 Tacoma Nature Center (Snake Lake)

DISTANCE:	About 2 miles of trails
ELEVATION GAIN:	Up to 110 feet
HIGH POINT:	420 feet
DIFFICULTY:	Easy
FITNESS:	Walkers, hikers, runners
FAMILY-FRIENDLY:	Yes, and some trails jogger-stroller and wheelchair accessible
DOG-FRIENDLY:	Prohibited
AMENITIES:	Nature center, nature playground, native plant garden, interpretive displays, restrooms, water
CONTACT/MAP:	Metro Parks Tacoma
GPS:	N 47 14.528, W 122 29.594
BEFORE YOU GO:	Trails open from 8:00 AM to half hour after sunset; free admission but donations accepted

GETTING THERE

Driving: From Tacoma, follow I-5 south to State Route 16. Then drive west on SR 16 for 2 miles to exit 2A. Now turn right onto S. 19th Street and continue east for 0.4 mile. Next, turn right onto S. Tyler Street and proceed for 0.1 mile. Turn left into Tacoma Nature Center for parking and trailhead.

Transit: Pierce Transit line 2.

Walk along, around, and across long, slender Snake Lake. Kids will especially love the lake's two long bridges providing excellent viewing of wildlife-rich waters. Then take to a series of trails on the wooded ridge above the lake. Explore a meadow, a small viewpoint—and definitely check out the nature center. And snakes? They're here—but the lake is named for its serpentine shape not for an abundance of the slithering reptile.

GET MOVING

The Tacoma Nature Center is usually bustling with visitors. Do check out the nature center's main building, with its exhibits, gift shop, and bookstore, and nearby Discovery Pond (a natural play area for children). The center hosts many programs

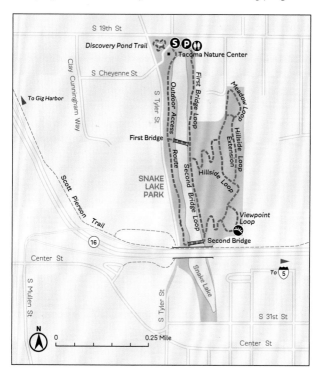

Bridge over Snake Lake

and classes (especially for children) throughout the year—check out its offerings on its website.

About 2 miles of trails branch out from the center's buildings, gardens, and playground. While trail running is allowed, it's best done elsewhere as the center's main purpose is for wildlife and wildlife observation. If you do choose to run here, be sure to adhere to the center's running rules.

The most popular trail route is the one-mile loop around nearly the whole serpentine lake. In 1972, SR 16 was constructed over the southern tip of the lake, so the trail doesn't completely encircle this small body of water. Being close to SR 16 also means that highway noise is a constant in the background over bird chatter and frog croaking. This loop includes a lake-spanning bridge near its southern end and another bridge spanning the lake midway. The best way to hike the loop is a figure eight. Enjoy the large cottonwoods and Garry oaks along the way. And from the bridges, look for wood ducks.

Add some extra mileage and a little elevation to your hike by adding on the Hillside Loop, which climbs a little more than

100 feet up the forested ridge to the lake's east. From this trail, there are three small loop options you can add on. The Hillside Extension Loop runs along the ridge traversing groves of stately, mature Douglas fir. The Meadow Loop circles around a small, old farm pasture. And the Viewpoint Loop leads to a madrona-ringed bluff above SR 16, where you can see Mount Rainier in the distance. Powerlines, however, interfere with getting a good photograph of the mountain. The beauty in this park is in the micro-delights: a frog surfacing in the reeds, ducks and geese wading placid waters, and fragrant woodland wildflower blossoms adding sweet scents to the air.

8 Wright Park

DISTANCE:	More than 2 miles of trails
ELEVATION GAIN:	Up to 50 feet
HIGH POINT:	320 feet
DIFFICULTY:	Easy
FITNESS:	Walkers, runners
FAMILY-FRIENDLY:	Yes, and some trails jogger-stroller and wheelchair accessible
DOG-FRIENDLY:	On leash
AMENITIES:	Restrooms, water, benches, interpretive displays, sculptures and statues, bocce ball green, playgrounds, "sprayground," botanical conservatory
CONTACT/MAP:	Metro Parks Tacoma
GPS:	N 47 15.642, W 122 26.856
BEFORE YOU GO:	Open from half hour before sunrise until half hour after sunset

GETTING THERE

Driving: From Tacoma, follow I-705 north and take the exit for Stadium Way just before the road becomes Schuster Parkway. Then turn right on S. Stadium Way and drive for 0.5 mile. Next turn left onto Division Avenue and continue for 0.3 mile.

Turn left onto S. I Street and park along the street for the park and trailhead. Additional street parking can also be found on S. G Street.

Transit: Pierce Transit lines 1, 11, and 16.

The closest thing to an East Coast city park in the Northwest, Wright Park in Tacoma's historic Stadium District feels like it could be in Boston, Philadelphia, or New York City. Huge eastern hardwoods, eloquent statues, a Victorian botanical conservatory, and a bocce ball green certainly help with the eastern feel. But there are plenty of touches of the Northwest here too in this beautifully landscaped and designed park. Enjoy a retreat from the bustling world with an invigorating run, afternoon walk, or an evening *passeggiata* (stroll) in this soothing park.

GET MOVING

While Wright Park is only 27 acres, it's packed with attractions, including more than six hundred fine trees, an array of statues and sculptures, and a pretty manmade pond graced with a fountain and spanned by a bridge. The park was established in 1886 through a donation by Charles B. Wright, president of the Tacoma Land Company. Wright commissioned Bavarian American landscape architect Edward Otto Schwagerl to design the park. Schwagerl (who later worked for the Seattle Parks Department) was greatly influenced by Frederick Law Olmsted, the father of American landscape architecture. Like Olmsted's famous Central Park in New York City, Wright Park was designed to offer weary urbanites a place to renew themselves.

Renew yourself by wandering along the park's more than 2 miles of well-groomed soft-surface trails. A loop path winds 0.9 mile around the park on a rolling landscape that was altered during the park's development. Lots of side paths radiate from the loop, leading to quiet corners and points of

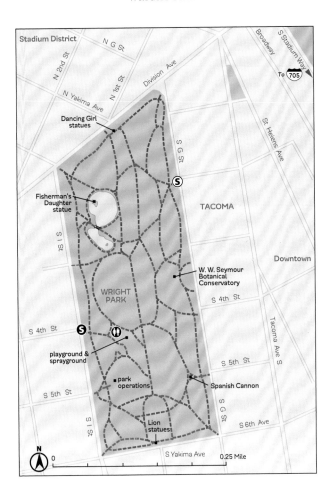

interest, like a cannon captured in Cuba during the Spanish-American War. You can walk or run for miles trying to cover them all in various loop arrangements.

A wide path cuts through the heart of the park. Lined with benches and big trees, it looks straight out of Europe or the East Coast. It was once part of Yakima Avenue, but in 1927 it

Dancing girl statue at old park entrance

was converted to trail. Its ends are graced with statues that once greeted motorists entering the park. Now children (and adults) can inspect the lions and dancing girls in a much more peaceful atmosphere.

The park is as much an arboretum as it is a place to rec-reate. Wright is graced with magnificent specimens of trees from the Northwest, East Coast, and Europe. Trees from South America and Asia were later added to the park. Many of the trees are labeled, and several of them have historical significance too, like the red oak planted in 1903 to commemorate President Theodore Roosevelt's visit to the city. There are eighteen champion trees within the park. These are trees that are the largest specimens of their kind in the state. Download a copy of the Champion Tree Tour brochure from the Metro Parks website to take with you on your visit so that you can locate and appreciate these significant trees.

You may also want to visit the 1907-built W. W. Seymour Botanical Conservatory (donation suggested) located within the park. This distinctive Victorian building, with its twelve-sided central dome, contains three thousand panes of glass and is listed on the National Historic Register. It houses more than five hundred species of plants within its collection. There is always something in bloom. And come May, rhododendrons within the park add another layer of beauty.

9   Wapato Park

DISTANCE:	About 2 miles of trails
ELEVATION GAIN:	Minimal
HIGH POINT:	340 feet
DIFFICULTY:	Easy
FITNESS:	Walkers, runners
FAMILY-FRIENDLY:	Yes, and some trails jogger-stroller and wheelchair accessible
DOG-FRIENDLY:	On-leash and off-leash areas
AMENITIES:	Restrooms, water, benches, picnic tables and shelter, playground
CONTACT/MAP:	Metro Parks Tacoma
GPS:	N 47 11.569, W 122 27.320
BEFORE YOU GO:	Open from half hour before sunrise until half hour after sunset

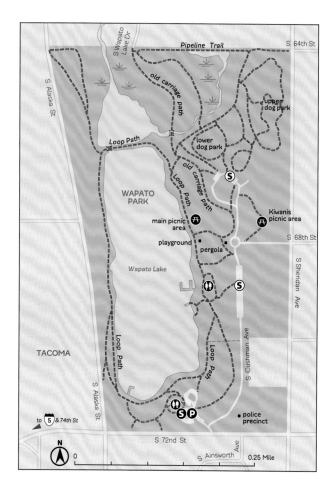

GETTING THERE

Driving: From Tacoma, follow I-5 south to exit 129. Then turn left onto S. 74th Street (which turns into 72nd) and proceed for 0.5 mile. Turn left onto S. Ainsworth Avenue and enter Wapato Park for parking and trailhead.

   Transit: Pierce Transit lines 48, 55, and 202.

Cottonwoods donning autumn foliage

Developed in the late 1880s as a private park and later enhanced in the 1930s by the Works Progress Administration (WPA), Wapato Park captures these two periods quite nicely. Stroll around Wapato Lake and through the surrounding grounds, admiring a beautiful pergola, historic boathouse, and an old carriage path. And while the lake is pretty, it's the park's trees that are really exceptional. Marvel at towering firs, cottonwoods, oaks, and ashes.

GET MOVING

When established by R. F. Radebaugh (owner of the *Tacoma Daily Ledger* newspaper) back in 1889, Wapato Park was far removed from the hustle and bustle of the city. Back then, folks would take a streetcar (owned by Radebaugh) and travel 6 miles to the private park. Today the park is located just minutes from I-5. While no longer a rural retreat, it still offers visitors a quiet place to take a break from urban living.

Acquired by Metro Parks in 1920, the 85-acre park has seen some nice improvements in the last few years, including renovations to its historic structures. And while wapato (an aquatic plant whose tubers were important to Native peoples) no longer flourish in the lake named for them, the water quality in this small spring-fed lake has greatly improved within the past two decades.

A 0.9-mile paved path loops the lake. Actually it cuts across the northern reaches of the lake on a dike and small bridge. Aside from plenty of views of the placid body of water are plenty of elegant trees—both hardwoods and softwoods line the path. The oaks, ash, cascara, and cottonwoods make this loop especially pretty in October. The lake is especially pretty too in the mornings and evenings when those magnificent trees reflect on, and light dances and twinkles upon, the lake's stilled waters.

Several paths with soft surfaces and hard surfaces depart the lake loop. You can walk along the lake's northern marshy shores and through a grove of old-growth conifers. Near the park's east entrance, an accessible path utilizes an old carriage path, passing by the beautiful flower-adorned park pergola, crossing a WPA bridge, and leading to S. Wapato Lake Drive. Here notice a trail that follows along a pipeline bridge. The path heads east and west and traverses a wetland pocket teeming with birds. The northeast end of the park contains a large dog park with short interconnecting trails.

10 Water Flume Line Trail

DISTANCE:	2.5 miles one-way
ELEVATION GAIN:	Minimal
HIGH POINT:	300 feet
DIFFICULTY:	Easy
FITNESS:	Walkers, runners, bikers
FAMILY-FRIENDLY:	Yes, and jogger-stroller and wheelchair accessible
DOG-FRIENDLY:	On leash
AMENITIES:	Restrooms, water, benches, playground, lighting, interpretive signs
CONTACT/MAP:	Metro Parks Tacoma
GPS:	N 47 12.716, W 122 28.932
BEFORE YOU GO:	South Park and Oak Tree Park open from half hour before sunrise until half hour after sunset

GETTING THERE

Driving: From Tacoma, follow I-5 south to exit 130. Then turn left on Tacoma Mall Boulevard and immediately turn right onto S. 56th Street. Continue 0.9 mile and turn right onto S. Tacoma Way. Then drive 0.4 mile and turn right onto S. 50th Street. Proceed 0.1 mile to South Park and trailhead. Parking available at Asia Pacific Cultural Center (in park) and along S. Puget Sound Avenue.

Transit: Pierce Transit lines 3, 53, and 202.

Though it is one of Tacoma's newest trails, the Water Flume Line is also one of the region's oldest trails. Walk or run on a reconstructed section of trail that was originally built in the 1890s and ran alongside an open wooden flume that provided water from Spanaway Lake to a reservoir in the new and growing city. Enjoy beautiful, rare Garry oaks and other stately trees gracing the two parks that this section of trail connects. The trail also passes by several historic homes and buildings as well as through South Park with its early-twentieth-century elegance.

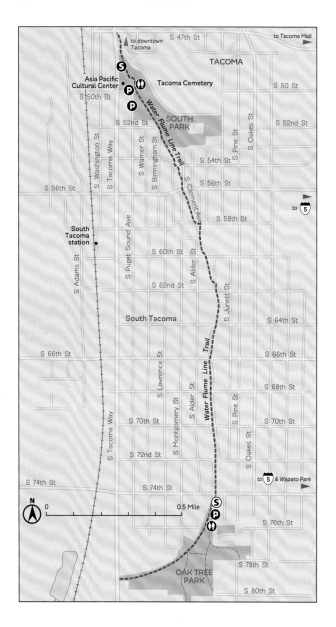

GET MOVING

The original Water Flume Line Trail stretched from Tacoma to the foothills of Mount Rainier. Much of it was composed of wooden planks with iron straps holding it together. It included a 405-foot-long bridge that spanned 105 feet above a gulch near Tacoma's Holy Rosary Church. The original water flume is long gone—replaced by pipelines and pump houses. In 2008 the city began to reconstruct a portion of the historic trail. Today 3.3 miles of the trail are open to pedestrians and cyclists. The plan is to eventually have a 6.5-mile trail in place, connecting neighborhoods in South Tacoma to downtown.

The trail currently exists in two unconnected segments. The 0.8-mile section of trail that travels primarily along S. Tacoma Way between S. M Street and S. C Street will appeal mainly to bicycle commuters. The 2.5-mile section described here, from just north of South Park to just south of Oak Tree Park, is a pure delight to walk or run.

Starting at the corner of S. Tacoma Way and S. 47th Street, the Water Flume Line Trail heads south through beautiful South Park, which was once part of the City of Tacoma Light and Water Company's waterline right-of-way and was made into a park in 1905. Graced with stately Douglas firs and Garry oaks, vintage lampposts, and a bandstand, the park has an early twentieth-century feel. The park is also home to the South Tacoma Community Center, which was originally built by the US Army during World War II as a United Services Organization facility. Today it is leased to the Asia Pacific Cultural Center.

The park is popular with people from all walks of life, and during hot summer days, folks take to its shaded lawns and spray park, also called a "sprayground." On hot days, reward any young walkers with a trip to the sprayground upon completion of your workout.

Beyond the park, the trail crosses a series of roads, with only a couple of them being heavily trafficked. Signals provide for safe passage. The trail passes through quiet neighborhoods

Black-eyed Susans line the Water Flume Line Trail.

and for a short stint runs parallel with S. Clement Avenue. The way passes by historic churches and schools that have served diverse populations and various immigrant communities over the decades.

South of 74th Street, the trail enters Oak Tree Park (an alternative starting point with parking and transit options). Here you will find restrooms and a water well that operates from 6:00 AM to 8:00 PM. Oak Tree Park was established in 1996 and protects a beautiful Garry oak forest within its 25 acres. Native from northern California to extreme southern Vancouver Island, this handsome hardwood has seen more than 90 percent of its range reduced. Interpretive signs identify the vegetation lining the trail through the park. In addition, about 0.75 mile of natural-surface trails also traverse the park. You can extend your walk or run by checking them out.

The Water Flume Line Trail continues a short distance, terminating at S. Tacoma Way near 80th Street Court SW. Here a couple of interpretive signs on the trail and waterline's history can be found.

11   Swan Creek Park

DISTANCE:	More than 5 miles of trails
ELEVATION GAIN:	Up to 350 feet
HIGH POINT:	390 feet
DIFFICULTY:	Easy to moderate
FITNESS:	Walkers, hikers, runners, bikers
FAMILY-FRIENDLY:	Yes, and some trails jogger-stroller and wheelchair accessible
DOG-FRIENDLY:	On leash
AMENITIES:	Privies, benches, picnic tables, community garden, mountain bike area
CONTACT/MAP:	Metro Parks Tacoma
GPS:	N 47 13.150, W 122 23.787
BEFORE YOU GO:	Open from half hour before sunrise until half hour after sunset

GETTING THERE

Driving: From Tacoma, follow I-705 south to State Route 7 until the freeway ends. Then head right (east) on E. 38th Street for 0.8 mile. Next, turn right onto Portland Avenue E. and drive 0.4 mile. Then turn left onto E. 44th Street and proceed 0.7 mile. Turn left onto E. Roosevelt Avenue and continue for 0.1 mile. Then turn right onto E. 42nd Street and drive into the park to parking area and trailhead.

Transit: Pierce Transit line 41.

One of Tacoma's larger parks, Swan Creek has two distinctive and interesting facades. The northern and eastern reaches of this 373-acre park consist of a deep forested ravine cradling cascading Swan Creek. The southern and western reaches of the park contain a mountain biking area and the intact road system of a former World War II housing development, once home to thousands. Hike the ravine—one of the wilder and more natural areas in the city—or stroll and run through a ghost neighborhood.

GET MOVING

Swan Creek Park has a long and fascinating history. Once threatened by mining, a landfill, and neglect, this park is now going through a revival with a lot of community support. A new trailhead with parking and picnicking, a community garden, mountain bike trail network, and the complete redevelopment of the surrounding neighborhood (once plagued with crime) has brought renewed interest to the park. Metro Parks continues to add amenities to this park and holds many family and community events (like fun runs) here.

Explore both the wild ravine housing the creek and the more developed and historic uplands west of the ravine all in one big day outing or on multiple trips. Many people intent on hiking the 2.4-mile Swan Creek Trail, which traverses a good part of the ravine, start at the trailhead located off of Pioneer Way. That trailhead, however, (managed by Pierce County Parks and Recreation) lacks amenities and maintenance and is a place where car prowls are a concern. If you park instead at E. 42nd Street, as indicated in the driving directions above, you can access the trail from one of the connectors coming off of the 1.2-mile Canyon Rim Trail.

Combining the Canyon Rim and Swan Creek Trails with one of the short connectors makes for a great lollipop loop and one of the best nature hikes in Tacoma. Both trails are described here: the Swan Creek Trail from north to south, and the Canyon Rim Trail from south to north.

The Swan Creek Trail's northern terminus begins on an old road near an old quarry. It then passes a small dammed area on Swan Creek (named for an early settler, not birds in the *Cygnus* genus) and enters the ravine, following alongside the tumbling creek. The trail then crosses the creek on a bridge and traverses the steep (and occasionally prone to washout) ravine slopes. The big conifers were removed from this valley long ago, but there are some big maples and cottonwoods along the way. The trail is in pretty decent shape, but the tread is narrow in

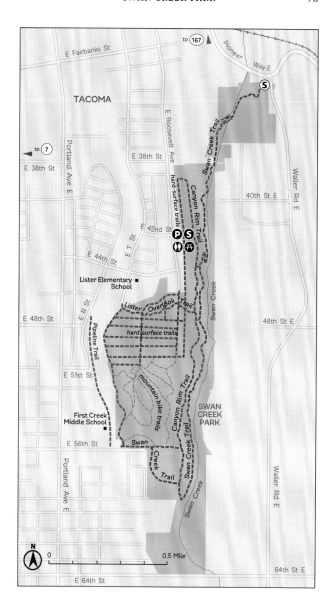

Bridge spanning Swan Creek

places and the slopes are steep, so keep kids and dogs close by. Pass three short connectors (all junctions marked with maps) to the Canyon Rim Trail above. The Swan Creek Trail continues up the ravine, bypassing an old slide area and then slowly making its way out of the ravine. The creek may be flowing underground along the trail's upper reaches. The trail then switchbacks and at 2.1 miles connects with the Canyon Rim Trail. The Swan Creek Trail continues 0.3 mile west to end at E. 56th Street.

The Canyon Rim Trail travels for 1.2 miles along the western rim of the ravine. It skirts the mountain bike trail system to the west. There are occasional views of the ravine and across it to a massive gravel quarry operation. The trail then skirts roads (now considered hard-surface trails) from the old Salishan housing development. It also intersects with the Lister Overlook Trail. This trail travels west across the old housing development site to terminate in 0.3 mile on E. T Street (street parking) near the Lister Elementary School. The Canyon Rim Trail then terminates at the E. 42nd Street Trailhead.

The hard-surface trails are perfect for running, biking, and jogger-strollers. This area was once part of the Salishan neighborhood, which was rapidly developed in the early 1940s to house workers during World War II. While it was designed to be a community, it was hastily built and many of the homes were shoddy and not meant to last. After the war, the neighborhood continued to grow and by 1950 comprised 6700 residents—more than half of them children. It was and still is one of the city's most diverse neighborhoods. It was also one of the city's poorer neighborhoods and was plagued by crime. By the 1980s, the neighborhood was in serious decline.

Through government programs and strong community involvement, all of the original homes (except for a handful kept and restored for historic preservation) were torn down in the early 2000s, and the Salishan neighborhood was completely redeveloped and revitalized. Crime plummeted and along with the resurrection of neighboring Swan Creek Park, the area began to flourish as a community.

GO FARTHER

From E. 56th Street, you can follow the more than 2-mile-long paved Pipeline Trail. Extended in 2018 to the Tacoma Dome, the trail will soon be expanded south to E. 72nd Street. Plans are to eventually have it connect with the Foothills Trail in Puyallup.

Next page: *Emerald Tunnel in Bresemann Forest*

LAKEWOOD AREA

Immediately to the south of Tacoma are the communities of Lakewood (Pierce County's second largest city), Steilacoom (Washington's first incorporated community), DuPont (site of one of Washington's oldest non-Native settlements), unincorporated Parkland and Spanaway, and the US military installation Joint Base Lewis-McChord. Once a wildlife-rich and biologically diverse expanse of lakes, prairies, and Garry oak forest, much of this area has been converted to industrial uses and suburban sprawl. And many of the remaining natural areas are being subdued by invasive species, especially the dreaded Scotch broom. While the area lacks many parks and trails, there are some gems within this region. The military installation protects large tracts of forest and prairies too, but these are closed to the public. Hopefully someday soon an abandoned rail line that crosses the base will be converted to trail and linked with a large trail system in Thurston County.

12 Farrell's Marsh Wildlife Area

DISTANCE:	About 1.5 miles of trails
ELEVATION GAIN:	Minimal
HIGH POINT:	260 feet
DIFFICULTY:	Easy
FITNESS:	Walkers, hikers
FAMILY-FRIENDLY:	Yes
DOG-FRIENDLY:	On leash
AMENITIES:	Map kiosk
CONTACT/MAP:	Town of Steilacoom Public Works; no map online
GPS:	N 47 09.865, W 122 35.763
BEFORE YOU GO:	Open from half hour before sunrise until half hour after sunset

GETTING THERE

Driving: From Tacoma, follow I-5 south to exit 124. Then turn right on Gravelly Lake Drive SW and proceed for 1.2 miles. Turn left onto Washington Boulevard SW and drive 1.2 miles, bearing right onto Military Road SW. Follow this road, which becomes Old Military Road in Steilacoom, for 1.6 miles. Then turn left onto Farrell Street and after 0.1 mile, turn right onto Stevens Street. Then in 0.1 mile turn left onto Beech Avenue and after 0.2 mile, turn left onto Chambers Street, immediately coming to the trailhead and limited roadside parking.

Transit: Pierce Transit line 212 stops at the corner of Sequalish and Chambers Streets, where it is a 0.3-mile walk south on quiet Chambers Street to the trailhead.

Wedged between historic Steilacoom and sprawling Joint Base Lewis-McChord is a natural little pocket of greenery. Here, walk a series of paths hugging marshy shoreline and traversing lush woodlands. Look for various birds among the reeds and thickets and for evidence of those who passed through this way before Washington achieved statehood.

GET MOVING

Steilacoom is a delightful little town perched on the shores of Puget Sound. Incorporated in 1854, Steilacoom is Washington's oldest incorporated community. Within the town are numerous historic buildings, including the state's oldest Catholic Church. At some point, definitely plan on walking around the town for some pleasant strolling. But first, head to Farrell's Marsh, located south of town.

The marsh is bordered by stately trees, including some madronas. Hazelnuts, spiraea, salal, and thickets of evergreen huckleberries also grace the shoreline. They provide great habitat for many of the marsh's birds (look for ducks, herons,

Quiet morning at Farrell's Marsh

and an occasional eagle), but make viewing the marsh's waters a challenge. There are, however, a couple of viewpoints allowing closer inspection of this wetland.

There are several trails within the park. None of them are signed, but finding your way around this small park isn't too challenging. Take a picture of the map at the trailhead kiosk, but note that it is missing a newer path in the park's southeast corner. You can hike a couple of short loops in the park, but you can't loop the marsh. Half of the marsh is located in the adjacent Joint Base Lewis-McChord. You'll come to a fence and might also hear rounds of artillery in the distance—a couple of clues not to trespass. A couple of trails head to neighborhood streets that are perfectly fine for looping back into the park.

The area is nearly level, and some of the trails are prone to flooding during really wet periods. However, there are a couple of bridges spanning the pair of creeks—one flowing in and one flowing out of the wetland. Within this property too are wagon ruts more than 150 years old. They are not signed, nor on the map. See if you can locate them. Steilacoom is packed with relics and remnants from Washington's territorial days.

13 **Fort Steilacoom Park**

DISTANCE:	More than 7 miles of trails
ELEVATION GAIN:	Up to 200 feet
HIGH POINT:	350 feet
DIFFICULTY:	Easy to moderate
FITNESS:	Walkers, hikers, runners, bikers
FAMILY-FRIENDLY:	Yes, and some trails wheelchair and jogger-stroller friendly
DOG-FRIENDLY:	On-leash and off-leash areas
AMENITIES:	Restrooms, water, picnic tables and shelters, playground, sports fields, historical sites and interpretation
CONTACT/MAP:	City of Lakewood Parks and Recreation
GPS:	N 47 10.367, W 122 33.626
BEFORE YOU GO:	Park open 7:30 AM to 9:00 PM or sunset (whichever comes first)

GETTING THERE

Driving: From Tacoma, follow I-5 south to exit 129. Then turn right onto S. 74th Street and proceed for 2.2 miles until the road bends to the south and becomes Custer Road W. Next continue straight on Custer Road W. for 1.2 miles, bearing right onto 88th Street SW. Proceed 0.3 mile, merging onto Steilacoom Boulevard SW. and continuing straight for 1 mile. Then turn left onto 87th Avenue SW and continue for 0.1 mile. Next turn right on Dresden Lane SW and enter Fort Steilacoom Park. Stay on Dresden for 0.7 mile to a large trailhead parking lot near the dog park entrance and historic barns.

Transit: Pierce Transit line 212.

A former army fort turned mental health hospital farm is now one of the largest and finest urban parks in the South Sound. Walk, run, or hike on miles of trails traversing woodlands, prairie, rolling hills, and lakeshore. Run and walk past structures and relics from the park's farm days. Saunter along

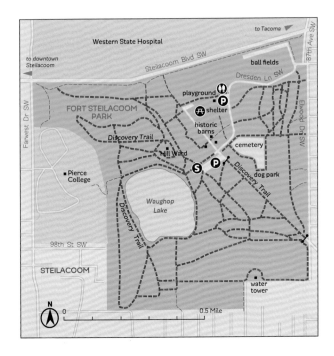

paved interpretive trails or just run or hike carefree on miles of
dirt trails. Delight at showy hardwoods reflecting in the park's
Waughop Lake, and marvel at Mount Rainier rising above that
placid body of water.

GET MOVING

Fort Steilacoom Park is a happening place with a long and colorful history. Dog lovers flock here to the park's large off-leash
dog park. Area runners regularly take to the park's paved and
dirt trails—and the park frequently hosts school cross-country
meets and community fun runs. The park is visited by history
fans, bird lovers, bicyclists, picnickers, and families for get-to-
gethers. But there is plenty of room to roam in this 340-acre

Mount Rainier hovers above Fort Steilacoom Park.

park, with many of the trails in the southern and western reaches of the park void of crowds.

If you're interested in a leisurely walk and learning about this park's fascinating history, follow the Discovery Trail. It's a route lined with interpretive signs and incorporating several of the park's paths, leading to historic structures and sites. The area was homesteaded in the 1840s and became part of

Fort Steilacoom (one of the first US military installations built north of the Columbia River) in 1849. Several of the fort's original buildings are still standing—located north of Steilacoom Boulevard SW and west of Western State Hospital.

In 1871, the fort was repurposed as a mental hospital, ultimately becoming Western State Hospital. A good portion of the original fort grounds south of Steilacoom Boulevard were operated as a farm for the hospital until 1965. Patients worked on the farm alongside staff. Several farm buildings are still standing, as well as the orchard.

If you're looking for easy running and walking routes, there are several level paved paths within the park, including a 1-mile trail along the park's northern border, a 0.6-mile path around the ball fields, and a 0.4-mile path along the dog park. The park has an established 5K running route too. The most popular trail within the park, however—and one you won't tire of walking or running—is the nearly level, 1.2-mile paved lollipop loop around Waughop Lake. Named for Doctor John Waughop, a former superintendent of the hospital, the lake is lined with stately ornamental trees, courtesy of Waughop's wife, Elizabeth. Admire them along the lake and elsewhere on the grounds. Lombardy poplars, sequoias, black locusts, sycamores, horse chestnuts, and other species grace the property.

From the lake loop, a paved path leads to the Hill Ward historic area. Here a large hospital ward once stood overlooking the lake. There are some interpretive displays here, as well as a labyrinth for meditation. Beyond Hill Ward, follow some soft-surface paths to an open hillside in the park's southwestern corner. Enjoy a breathtaking view of Mount Rainier rising above the grounds, as well as views of the Cascades, Olympics, and McNeil and Fox Islands.

North of this hill, trails lead to the adjacent Pierce College and then to forested and grassy slopes along the park's southern reaches. In the park's eastern reaches, find a series of trails traversing patches of remnant prairie and oak groves. Unfortunately, invasive Scotch broom is choking out prairie plants in parts of the park. Hopefully volunteers can eradicate this pox on the land in this beautiful and culturally and naturally significant park.

14 Spanaway Park and Bresemann Forest

DISTANCE:	More than 5 miles of trails
ELEVATION GAIN:	Minimal
HIGH POINT:	350 feet
DIFFICULTY:	Easy
FITNESS:	Walkers, runners, bikers
FAMILY-FRIENDLY:	Yes, and some trails wheelchair and jogger-stroller friendly
DOG-FRIENDLY:	On leash
AMENITIES:	Restrooms, water, picnic tables and shelters, playground, sports fields, swimming area
CONTACT/MAP:	Pierce County Parks and Recreation
GPS:	N 47 07.311, W 122 26.746
BEFORE YOU GO:	Parking fees are in effect from mid-May until Labor Day; park open 6:30 AM to dusk; seasonal parking lot closures during the holiday season

GETTING THERE

Driving: From Tacoma, follow I-5 south to exit 127. Then follow State Route 512 east for 0.7 mile, taking the Steele Street exit. Turn left and follow Steele Street S., which becomes 116th Street S. after 0.5 mile. Continue 0.3 mile on 116th Street S., which then becomes Spanaway Loop Road S., and drive 1.9 miles. Then turn left onto Military Road S. and proceed for 0.6 mile. Next turn right onto Bresemann Boulevard S. and enter Spanaway Park, continuing to parking lots and trailheads within the park.

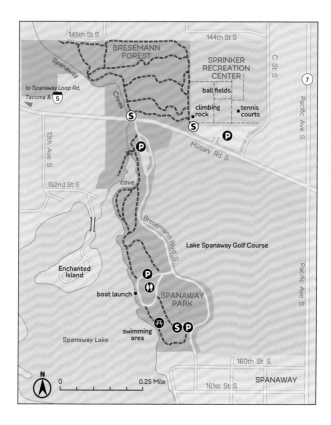

Transit: Pierce Transit line 1 stops at the junction of Military Road S. and Pacific Avenue S. (State Route 7), from where it is a 0.4-mile walk along Military Road S. to Bresemann Forest Trailhead at the Sprinker Recreation Center.

Your choice: paved trails on manicured grounds along rolling lakeshore, or nearly level soft-surface paths in a quiet natural forest. Adjoining Spanaway Park and Bresemann Forest offer contrasting experiences on their more than 5 miles of combined trails. These two parks—one along the eastern shore of

Quiet cover on Spanaway Lake

Spanaway Lake and one embracing Spanaway Creek—both offer some pleasant surprises and excellent walking and running opportunities beyond Parkland's urban sprawl.

GET MOVING

The 135-acre Spanaway Park can be a busy place during the warm days of summer, when hundreds upon hundreds of folks flock here to play in Spanaway Lake. During the off-season, however, the park can be pretty sedate. More than half of this park consists of a golf course. The other half contains a beach, picnic areas, and parking lots. But between the park road and lakeshore are several miles of interconnecting paved paths. They run over rolling lawns and through groves of towering Douglas firs. They'll take you along the lake and to a small cove that is graced with dogwoods and Oregon ash and usually flourishing with birds and other critters.

From the park's northernmost parking lot to its southernmost is a distance of about a mile. It's easy to walk or run 3 miles here by doing an out-and-back and a couple of side loops. At the park's northern reaches, Spanaway Creek flows from the lake. Here a soft-surface path takes off west, crossing the creek on a pair of bridges and then meandering through forest. The trail eventually grows brushier and leaves the park.

The 70-acre Bresemann Forest can be reached by carefully crossing Military Road near the Spanaway Park entrance and entering through a gate. Bresemann can also be accessed from a trailhead to the east near the Sprinker Recreation Center. This is a good place to park too if you just want to walk the forest trails and avoid paying the summer day-use fee at Spanaway Park.

Within this tract of wild forest are about 2 miles of interconnecting trails. There are no trail markers or signs.

A wide, well-trodden trail travels close to the periphery of the forest, which is bordered by Spanaway Creek on the west, ball fields from the Sprinker Recreation Center on the east, and gates north and south. It's about a mile to walk the periphery. There is an orienteering course in the forest and a climbing rock near the Sprinker entrance. The forest is quite attractive as is the stretch along Spanaway Creek, where you'll come upon an old mill dam and a newer bypass channel for native fish. The creek was first dammed here back in the 1870s by German immigrant Gustav Bresemann.

Bresemann eventually sold his land claim on Spanaway Lake to the Tacoma Light and Power Company, which opened Spanaway Park in the early 1900s. His family retained the forest until the 1960s, when it was sold to Pierce County Parks and Recreation. There are many mature trees within the forest and a luxuriant understory of vine maples and other shrubs. Except for some street noise and planes flying overhead from Joint Base Lewis-McChord, the area retains a look and feel that Bresemann, if he were alive today, would recognize.

| 15 | **Sequalitchew Creek Trail** |

DISTANCE:	3.2 miles roundtrip
ELEVATION GAIN:	225 feet
HIGH POINT:	225 feet
DIFFICULTY:	Moderate
FITNESS:	Hikers, runners
FAMILY-FRIENDLY:	Yes
DOG-FRIENDLY:	On leash
AMENITIES:	Restrooms, picnic tables, interpretive signs
CONTACT/MAP:	City of DuPont Parks and Recreation
GPS:	N 47 06.370, W 122 38.754

GETTING THERE

Driving: From Tacoma, follow I-5 south to exit 118. Keep right at the fork and proceed on Center Drive for 1.2 miles. Next, turn left onto Civic Drive and proceed for 0.1 mile. Then turn right into the parking lot near City Hall, the fire department, and police department. The trailhead is located just north of City Hall.

Follow a small creek from a remnant prairie, down a narrow ravine, to a secluded beach on Puget Sound's Nisqually Reach. En route, stop at relics and interpretive displays highlighting this region's fascinating history. This short trail travels through time—from a Nisqually people's winter village, to a Hudson's Bay Company fort, to a DuPont explosives factory, to a planned development—and gives intriguing insights into the past.

GET MOVING

The trail starts next to DuPont City Hall and Civic Center. Stop at interpretive displays as you work your way across a fragment of the prairies that once were common across the South Sound region. The trail then takes a left and comes to an old flume dam at the edge of a forest of Douglas firs and

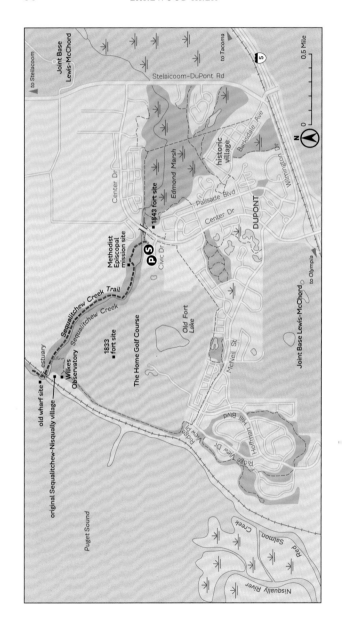

Garry oaks. The flume dam was once used to provide power to the lower powerhouse—more about that later.

The trail then passes the site of a short lived Methodist Episcopal mission. Established in 1839, the mission was the first American settlement on Puget Sound. The trail becomes paved and, utilizing an old narrow-gauge railroad bed, begins to descend into the ravine cut by Sequalitchew Creek. In 1906, the DuPont Company bought much of the surrounding land and built an explosives factory where the Home Golf Course now sits. The railroad, known as the Dynamite Train, transported the explosives down to a dock on the sound and brought materials back up to the factory.

The trail resumes as a gravel path and, at 1.25 miles, comes to a junction near where the old lower powerhouse—used to produce electricity for DuPont's factory and company town—once stood. The trail left (see Go Farther) climbs out of the ravine and offers a historic and scenic extension to this trip.

The main trail continues straight, coming to a small estuary (watch for myriad bird species) before entering a graffiti-laden tunnel under an active set of railroad tracks. The trail then emerges on Puget Sound, where you can continue right a short distance to a gravel beach, passing the remains of the old DuPont wharf, which once reached 300 feet into the sound. Look for seals and sea birds. And enjoy views out to Anderson, Ketron, Fox, and McNeil Islands.

GO FARTHER

Extend your hike and visit more historical sites by following the trail by the old powerhouse site. Utilizing switchbacks, it makes a steep but short climb of about 175 feet out of the ravine. At about 0.25 mile, it reaches the Wilkes Observatory, which commemorates American Naval Officer Charles Wilkes's expedition visit in 1841 (see sidebar). From this post, enjoy good views over the Sequalitchew Creek Estuary. It was

Madronas and firs line the bluff top trail near the Wilkes Observatory.

here that, for many years, a Nisqually winter village consisting of two longhouses once stood.

The trail now continues southwest on a high bluff above the sound, paralleling an old industrial site consumed by Scotch broom. It was not too far from here that in 1833, the Hudson's Bay Company established Fort Nisqually, a fur-trading post and the first non-Native settlement on Puget Sound. The fort operated until 1869. In the 1930s, the fort was rebuilt in Point Defiance Park (see Trail 3). Two of the original buildings remain, and the entire complex is open to the public as a living history museum.

The trail continues along the bluff, passing through a tunnel of trees. Pass by some beautiful madronas, oaks, and excellent viewing points over the sound. The way rolls a little before bending left and terminating at 1.4 miles at Ridge View Place, a housing development. You can return the way you came, or loop back to your start via 2 miles of paved trails and sidewalks (be sure to pick up or download a city trails map). The city has more than 12 miles of trails to explore. The paths leading to and across the Edmond Marsh are worth checking out.

LIEUTENANT CHARLES WILKES AND THE UNITED STATES EXPLORING EXPEDITION

When it comes to early Pacific Northwest explorers and their impact on mapping and studying the region, most folks are familiar with Captain George Vancouver and with Lewis and Clark's Corps of Discovery. Many folks, however, know little to nothing about the United States Exploring Expedition led by Lieutenant Charles Wilkes from 1838 to 1842. Known as the Wilkes Expedition, the US Navy lieutenant spent four years exploring the Pacific Ocean, including time in Puget Sound. He was responsible for naming many of the region's landmarks, often after his crew members.

He was born in New York City in 1798 and was raised by his aunt, Elizabeth Ann Seton, who later was canonized as the first Catholic saint born in the United States. His journey in 1838 was the first US Navy expedition in the Pacific. He departed Virginia, commanding six vessels with a crew that included experts in several disciplines. He surveyed Antarctica and visited Fiji and the Hawaiian Islands. His expedition kidnapped Fijian chief Vendovi (for which an island in Skagit County is named) for murdering a crew of American whalers. Wilkes also had eighty Fijians killed as retribution for the deaths of two of his sailors, one of whom was his nephew.

In the spring of 1841, he commenced a detailed survey of Puget Sound. He ended up naming or renaming scores of landmarks, including the following: Agate Passage, Anderson Island, Budd Inlet, Dana Passage, Elliott Bay, Hale Passage, Hammersley Inlet, Maury Island, McNeil Island, Port Ludlow, and Quartermaster Harbor. He held the first American Independence Day celebration west of the Mississippi River in DuPont on July 5, 1841. The area was then part of Oregon Country, jointly administered with the United Kingdom.

When the expedition finished, Wilkes had logged 87,000 miles and lost two ships and twenty-eight men. He was court-martialed for the loss of one ship, the massacre of eighty Fijians, and for the harsh treatment of his subordinates and mistreatment and harsh punishment (which included lashing with a cat-o'-nine-tails whip) of his sailors. He was acquitted of most of the charges. He later commanded a ship in the American Civil War and attacked a British ship, nearly leading to a war between the United States and the United Kingdom. Many scholars believe that Wilkes was used as the prototype for Captain Ahab in Herman Melville's *Moby Dick*. Wilkes died in 1877, and his remains now rest in the Arlington National Cemetery.

Next page: *Staircase leading to Nisqually Reach Aquatic Reserve*

ANDERSON ISLAND

Naval officer Charles Wilkes named Anderson Island after Alexander Caulfield Anderson, the chief trader at the nearby Hudson's Bay Company's Fort Nisqually. The name seemed apropos as a wave of settlers of Scandinavian descent came to the island a few decades later. Connected to the mainland by the Pierce County Ferry, Anderson Island is the southernmost island in Puget Sound. With a year-round population of around 2000, much of the island retains a rural charm. Be sure to visit the historic Johnson Farm Museum. Built in 1896, the restored farm and grounds are operated by the Anderson Island Historical Society and give a nice glimpse into the island's past. Then take to several miles of trails on the island's growing system of parks and nature preserves.

16 Jane Cammon and Montalvo Parks

DISTANCE:	1.5 miles of trails
ELEVATION GAIN:	Up to 200 feet
HIGH POINT:	275 feet
DIFFICULTY:	Easy to moderate
FITNESS:	Walkers, hikers, runners, bikers
FAMILY-FRIENDLY:	Yes
DOG-FRIENDLY:	On leash
AMENITIES:	Privy, picnic table, playground
CONTACT/MAP:	Anderson Island Park and Recreation District
GPS:	N 47 09.780, W 122 42.834

GETTING THERE

Driving: From Tacoma, follow I-5 south to exit 129. Then turn right onto S. 74th Street and proceed for 2.2 miles until the road bends to the south and becomes Custer Road W. Next continue straight on Custer Road W. for 1.2 miles, bearing right onto 88th Street SW. Proceed 0.3 mile, merging onto Steilacoom Boulevard SW. and continuing straight 3 miles to Steilacoom. Then continue on an arterial (Puyallup Street, which becomes Rainier Street) for 0.5 mile and turn right on Union Avenue and drive 0.2 mile to the ferry terminal.

After the crossing, continue west from the Anderson Island Ferry Terminal on Yoman Road for 0.8 mile, bearing left onto Eckenstam Johnson Road. Continue 0.7 mile and turn right onto Lake Josephine Boulevard and proceed 0.4 mile to four-way junction. Proceed straight on Camus Road for 0.4 mile to parking and trailhead on your right, near a playfield.

Walk or run on quiet trails on a hillside shrouded with stately second-growth forest and thick patches of evergreen huckleberries and salal. These two small parks, along with an

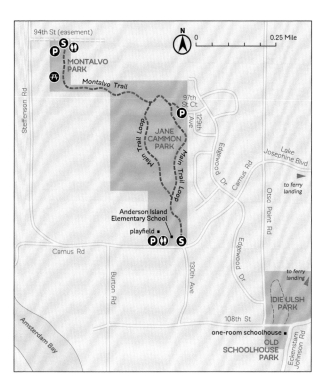

adjoining Pierce County parcel, provide more than 60 acres to roam. And unlike other parks on the island, the higher ground here means that these trails don't flood during Anderson Island's rainy season.

GET MOVING

Jane Cammon was a teacher and illustrator from a family with long ties to Anderson Island. She passed away in 1996, and this park was named in her honor. Montalvo Park was a gift to the island from Steve Montalvo in memory of his parents. The two parks are connected by a trail that traverses a

Thick salal understory in uniform fir forest

large tract owned by Pierce County. The Anderson Island Park and Recreation District would like to develop more trails on that tract someday. For now, you have your pick between two.

The Main Trail Loop takes off from just east of the elementary school (a short walk from the parking area). Follow it 0.1 mile before it loops 1 mile. This wide trail cuts through a thick forest understory, and elevation gain is pretty minimal. There are some bike trails complete with jumps that cut across the loop. You'll want to stick to the main walking path.

There is a 0.1-mile path that leaves the loop east for a trailhead and parking area on 97th Street Court. And there is a newer trail that leaves west from the loop. You'll want to check out that one—the Montalvo Trail travels 0.4 mile to Montalvo Park (which has parking and is reached from 94th Street.). This trail drops about 80 feet as it cuts through a uniform forest of fir and dense thickets of salal and evergreen huckleberry. Combine an out-and-back on this trail with the main trail for a 2-mile walk or run.

GO FARTHER

Not too far from Jane Cammon Park is Old Schoolhouse Park. Definitely explore the one-room schoolhouse (oldest in Pierce County), which is on the National Register of Historic Places and is now used as a community exercise facility. Across the street from the schoolhouse is Anderson Island's newest park, Idie Ulsh, named after a co-founder of the Washington Butterfly Association. There are a few short trails within this small 16-acre park. Check them out as they traverse a grove of some of the biggest cedars on the island and make a bridged crossing of Schoolhouse Creek near its headwaters.

17 Andy's Marine Park

DISTANCE:	1.5-miles roundtrip
ELEVATION GAIN:	190 feet
HIGH POINT:	170 feet
DIFFICULTY:	Moderate
FITNESS:	Hikers
FAMILY-FRIENDLY:	Yes
DOG-FRIENDLY:	Prohibited
AMENITIES:	Privy, bike rack
CONTACT/MAP:	Anderson Island Park and Recreation District
GPS:	N 47 08.980, W 122 43.371

GETTING THERE

Driving: From Tacoma, follow I-5 south to exit 129. Then turn right onto S. 74th Street and proceed for 2.2 miles until the road bends to the south and becomes Custer Road W. Next continue straight on Custer Road W. for 1.2 miles, bearing right onto 88th Street SW. Proceed 0.3 mile, merging onto Steilacoom Boulevard SW. and continuing straight 3 miles to Steilacoom. Then continue on an arterial (Puyallup Street, which becomes Rainier Street) for 0.5 mile and turn right on Union Avenue and drive 0.2 mile to the ferry terminal.

After the crossing, continue west from the Anderson Island Ferry Terminal on Yoman Road for 0.8 mile, bearing left onto Eckenstam Johnson Road. Continue 1.4 miles and turn right onto Sandberg Road. Then drive 0.8 mile and turn left onto Claussen Road. Continue 0.4 mile to parking and trailhead on your right.

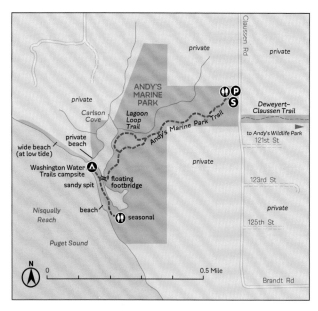

Hike from a forested bluff to a hidden cove lined with old-growth firs and mature madronas. Then walk across the cove on a floating bridge to a sandy spit. Marvel at wonderful maritime views across the Nisqually Reach out to the Olympic Mountains and Mount Rainier. And when the tide is low, wander along 0.75 mile of public beach, often littered with scads of sand dollars.

Floating bridge over lagoon near trail's end

GET MOVING

A gift to the people of Anderson Island from Andrew Anderson, an island pioneer and founding commissioner of the island's park and recreation district, this now nearly 90-acre park is a South Sound gem. Start your hike on a wide and well-maintained trail. It travels through an impressive forest that includes Oregon ash and some large madronas. Thick rows of evergreen huckleberries line the way. The trail steadily loses elevation, coming to a junction at 0.4 mile. Go either way; it's a loop and return the way you didn't go on the way in. The trail to the right—the Lagoon Loop Trail—is a little longer than the way to the left, adding just 0.1 mile to your hike.

The Lagoon Loop Trail passes through a grove of old-growth trees, then teeters on a bluff above Carlson Cove. Look for eagles in the surrounding trees or fishing for salmon below in the lagoon. The two trails then meet back up, and the main trail makes a short little climb before steeply descending to the cove. Here a floating bridge aided by pontoons will help get you safely across the cove to a sandy spit on the Nisqually Reach. A short path leads left along the spit, offering good cove views. Find here too, on the spit, Washington Water Trails Association campsites (reserved through the park district) for kayakers and canoeists.

Lounge around the sandy and cobbled beach and enjoy good views out to Mount Rainier, the Olympics, and Johnson Point. Tolmie State Park lies directly across the reach. If the tide is low, cross the cove outlet (which will get your shoes wet, but it's easily navigable) and walk north along a wide and mainly cobbled beach. Most of the way is below bluffs. The beach is public for 0.75 mile, but the surrounding uplands is private, so respect all property postings. Watch for seals and a wide array of birds, and watch your step as you walk across flats often teeming with live sand dollars.

18   Andy's Wildlife Park

DISTANCE:	2.1 miles of trails
ELEVATION GAIN:	Up to 160 feet
HIGH POINT:	150 feet
DIFFICULTY:	Easy
FITNESS:	Hikers
FAMILY-FRIENDLY:	Yes
DOG-FRIENDLY:	On leash
AMENITIES:	Privy, picnic table
CONTACT/MAP:	Anderson Island Park and Recreation District
GPS:	N 47 09.118, W 122 42.486
BEFORE YOU GO:	North half of Andy's Wildlife Trail prone to flooding from November through April

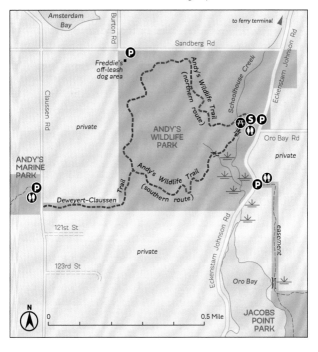

GETTING THERE

Driving: From Tacoma, follow I-5 south to exit 129. Then turn right onto S. 74th Street and proceed for 2.2 miles until the road bends to the south and becomes Custer Road W. Next continue straight on Custer Road W. for 1.2 miles, bearing right onto 88th Street SW. Proceed 0.3 mile, merging onto Steilacoom Boulevard SW. and continuing straight 3 miles to Steilacoom. Then continue on an arterial (Puyallup Street, which becomes Rainier Street) for 0.5 mile and turn right on Union Avenue and drive 0.2 mile to the ferry terminal.

After the crossing, continue west from the Anderson Island Ferry Terminal on Yoman Road for 0.8 mile, bearing left onto Eckenstam Johnson Road. Then continue 1.6 miles to parking and trailhead on your right.

The largest park on little Anderson Island, Andy's Wildlife Park offers excellent hiking and wonderful wildlife viewing. This 170-acre park sits in the heart of the island, protecting tidal flats and pine and fir groves. Enjoy wandering on a nearly level, almost 2-mile loop around the park. Then add a little elevation gain to your hike by taking to a trail that heads for higher ground.

GET MOVING

A good portion of this park contains salt flats along School-house Creek, close to where it empties into Oro Bay. It is rich estuarine habitat—but also, being at an elevation near sea level, prone to flooding. The park is open year-round, but the northern half of the loop can get quite soggy half of the year. During those rainy months, consider wearing good waterproof boots.

From the parking lot, locate Andy's Wildlife Trail. Either direction will work for this delightful 1.8-mile loop. The northern section is wide and practically flat, cutting though a grove of shore pines and thickets of evergreen huckleberries. The southern section wiggles a little more and crosses the tidal flats, making two bridged crossings of Schoolhouse Creek and a tributary. Look for herons and eagles here—and salmon. The parks district, with the help of grants and volunteers, has restored the creek in the park to its original course. All involved are hoping to see chum salmon runs return to this creek.

Taking off from the loop (1 mile from the trailhead via the northern section, and 0.8 mile via the southern section) is the Deweyert-Claussen Trail. This path climbs one hundred feet or so, traversing a hillside via an easement granted by Delbert and Janice Deweyert. The path ends in 0.4 mile on Claussen Road (no parking). From here you can walk north on this quiet rural road 0.1 mile and reach Andy's Marine Park (Trail 17), allowing you to make your hike an all-day adventure if you care to.

Dogs are welcome on the Andy's Wildlife Park trails, but they need to be leashed as this park is mainly managed for wildlife habitat. There is, however, a 1-acre off-leash dog park within the park, accessible via Sandberg Road.

Old-growth firs in Andy's Wildlife Park

19 Jacobs Point Park

DISTANCE:	2.5-mile loop
ELEVATION GAIN:	Minimal
HIGH POINT:	40 feet
DIFFICULTY:	Easy
FITNESS:	Hikers
FAMILY-FRIENDLY:	Yes
DOG-FRIENDLY:	Prohibited
AMENITIES:	Privy, picnic tables, interpretive signs
CONTACT/MAP:	Anderson Island Park and Recreation District
GPS:	N 47 08.965, W 122 42.430

GETTING THERE

Driving: From Tacoma, follow I-5 south to exit 129. Then turn right onto S. 74th Street and proceed for 2.2 miles. Next continue straight on Custer Road W. for 1.2 miles, bearing right onto 88th Street SW. Proceed 0.3 mile, merging onto Steilacoom Boulevard SW. and continuing straight 3 miles to Steilacoom. Then continue on arterial (Puyallup Street, which becomes Rainier Street) for 0.5 mile and turn right on Union Avenue and drive 0.2 mile to the ferry terminal.

After the crossing, continue west from the Anderson Island Ferry Terminal on Yoman Road for 0.8 mile, bearing left onto Eckenstam Johnson Road. Then continue 1.8 miles to parking and trailhead on your left.

One of the largest protected marine parks on the South Sound, Jacobs Point is also one of the island's prettiest spots. Occupying 100 acres of a peninsula in Oro Bay, Jacobs Point contains a historic homestead, mature forests that include rare Garry oaks, wildlife-rich wetlands, an extensive beach, and sweeping views. Come on a clear day and be blown away at the view of Mount Rainier across the Nisqually Reach.

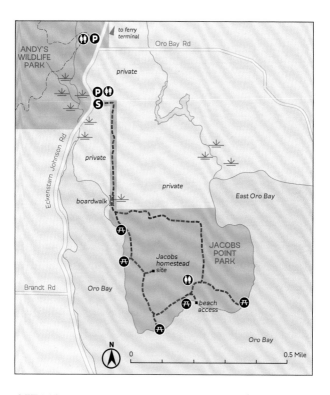

GET MOVING

Jacobs Point was purchased from Young Life (a Christian ministry for youth) in 2011 by Forterra (Washington's largest conservation and stewardship organization) with the help of several conservation funds. In 2016, Forterra purchased an additional 18 acres and added it to the park, allowing for the construction of a loop trail. The park contains 1 mile of protected beach and some of the best wildlife habitat on the island. Be sure to bring your binoculars along—the marsh, shoreline, and wetlands in the park are literally hopping with amphibians and teeming with small mammals and birds.

Hikers looking for wildlife in a wetland

The trail starts on an easement heading east, then makes a straight shot south. Cross a marsh on a boardwalk and then enter the park and come to a junction. This is the start of the loop. Head either direction, but the way right is more scenic, hugging the shoreline of Oro Bay and coming to a pair of viewpoints with picnic tables.

The way then turns a little inland and comes to a short spur leading to the old Jacobs homestead. Claude and Maude Jacobs built their house here in 1916. Jacobs cleared land that formerly was part of a brickyard for farming. The house was occupied on and off until 1980. By the 1990s, it collapsed. All that remains is the large chimney before you.

From here, the loop trail moves closer to the shore again, passing two more viewpoints with picnic tables. Admire, too, the forest you are hiking through. Among maturing firs are stately madronas and a few big Garry oaks. The trail then passes a stairway leading to the beach. During low tide, feel free to explore the beach. While there are good strands of sand and cobbled rocks, be aware of pockets of "sucking mud."

From the stairway, the trail continues, passing a composting toilet and coming to a junction. The loop heads left to return to the junction near the boardwalk. But first, head right on the spur trail leading to a bluff. Here, when the weather is good, is a grand view of Mount Rainier. The waters you are looking out across are part of the Nisqually Reach Aquatic Reserve, one of eight such reserves managed by the Washington Department of Natural Resources. These reserves are managed to preserve, restore, and enhance aquatic ecosystems that are of special educational, scientific, and environmental interest. A preserved Jacobs Point helps ensure that the waters surrounding it will continue to provide exceptional aquatic habitat.

Next page: *Trail traverses ravine cradling Hylebos Creek.*

FEDERAL WAY

Named after the old Federal Highway 99 (now State Route 99), Federal Way was incorporated in 1990 and has seen explosive growth in the last several decades. Though the city borders Tacoma, it is located in King County, and with a population just shy of 100,000, Federal Way is Washington's ninth largest city. The city was home to timber giant Weyerhaeuser for many decades, but in 2016 the company left its sprawling campus, which included open space that was open to the public, and moved to Seattle. Many folks in Federal Way are working to preserve the campus's open space—a rare commodity in urbanizing southern King County—as a park. Fortunately this city also has several other large greenbelts, including a more than 460-acre state park on Puget Sound. While much of Federal Way and its neighboring communities are bursting with housing developments, strip malls, apartment complexes, and big box stores, glimpses of farms and forests from a pre-I-5 Washington can be found here along the sound and in the Hylebos Creek Valley.

20 Dash Point State Park

DISTANCE:	More than 10 miles of trails
ELEVATION GAIN:	Up to 475 feet
HIGH POINT:	475 feet
DIFFICULTY:	Easy to moderate
FITNESS:	Walkers, hikers, runners, bikers
FAMILY-FRIENDLY:	Yes, but note some trails are heavily used by bikers
DOG-FRIENDLY:	On leash
AMENITIES:	Restrooms, campground, picnic tables and shelters
CONTACT/MAP:	Washington State Parks
GPS:	N 47 08.965, W 122 42.430
BEFORE YOU GO:	Discover Pass required

GETTING THERE

Driving: From Tacoma, follow State Route 509 (Marine View Drive in Northeast Tacoma) north for 11.4 miles. Then turn left into Dash Point State Park and drive 0.4 mile to a large parking area at the beach day-use area.

From Seattle follow I-5 south to exit 143. Then drive west on S 320th Street for 6.2 miles. Next turn right onto 47th Ave SW and drive for 0.4 mile. Then turn left onto SR 509 and continue 0.9 mile. Then turn right in Dash Point State Park and drive 0.4 mile to large parking area at beach day-use area.

Transit: King County Metro line 187 stops at the Hoyt Road SW Trailhead, at the east end of the park.

Hike, run, or walk more than 10 miles of trails in more than 460 acres of greenery wedged between Tacoma and Federal Way. Trails wind through ravines that cradle cascading creeks, and travel along thickly forested ridges. Most folks visit this popular park's 3300-foot beach, often leaving the trails pretty quiet. But definitely don't skip the beach—especially during a low tide, when you can roam a long way on extensive sandy tidal flats.

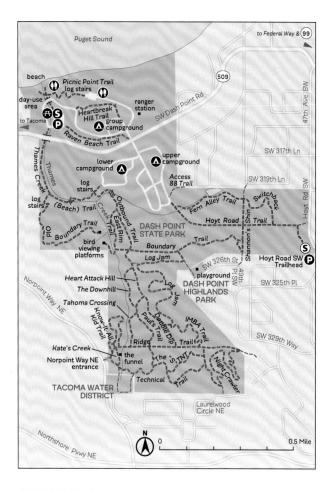

GET MOVING

The short path that heads north from the large day-use area parking lot is the path to Dash Point's large beach, and it's where most folks will be heading. Near the parking lot's entrance is the trailhead for the Thames Creek (Beach) Trail. This is your trailhead if you're looking to do some hiking or running.

Elaborate bridge over Thames Creek

You can get to just about all of the park's trails via this trail. Dash Point's trail system is pretty extensive. Many of the trails are signed, but you definitely want to take along a map. There's a good one with mileage on the state park's website. Also note that, generally, the lower trails are pedestrian-only, while the upper trails allow mountain bikes. The mountain bike trails are open to hikers and runners too, but they can get busy with bikers on weekends. Thick vegetation and tight turns can make visibility tough—so be aware of bikes and opt for quieter times.

The Thames Creek Trail travels for just shy of a half mile, following alongside Thames Creek in a deep emerald ravine. En route, it crosses the creek on a large and elaborate bridge sure to fascinate young hikers. Look, too, for big springboard-notched cedar stumps. Loggers of yesteryear stood on elevated planks (springboards) placed high in the trunks of big trees to make it easier to cut them down. The trail also connects the park's campground to the day-use area, making it a popular beeline to the beach for campers.

The Old Boundary Trail takes off from the Thames Creek Trail and, with its steps and steep climb out of the ravine, makes for a good workout. Unfortunately you have to hike it out and back until they replace a damaged bridge spanning a creek in a tight ravine.

The Boundary Trail (which follows the old boundary of the park) can be reached from either the Outbound Trail or East Rim Trail. It connects to a series of trails in the park's eastern reaches. Here trails connect to a couple of neighborhoods as well as a trailhead parking area (alternative start) on Hoyt Road SW. You can also loop back to the park's campground here by following either the Hoyt Road Trail or the hiker-only Fern Alley Trail, which also passes a very small pond surrounded by some big cottonwoods.

South of the Boundary Trail, several trails (all open to bikes) climb the upper slopes of the park and connect to even more trails. Many of these trails are flowy. They are fun to run when not too busy with bikes. The Ridge Trail is an old logging road that traverses the hillside for a fairly level route of 0.6 mile. It is one of the easier of the upper trails. The forest shrouding the upper trails was logged much later than the lower slopes of the park. Here you'll find primarily Douglas firs and big-leaf maples flourishing. Unfortunately there is quite a bit of invasive ivy flourishing in the park too, near the Norpoint Way NE entrance.

The Norpoint Way NE entrance is also close to "the funnel," an interesting relic left over from when this part of the park was once used for industrial purposes. A couple of trails branch from this region to pass through land owned by the Tacoma Water District. Be sure to stay on the trail here.

There are a couple of short trails that leave from the beach area too—both of them steep, allowing for some good conditioning if you run them. And if you want to go for endurance, a run or hike around the periphery of the park will yield around 6 miles and a good bit of elevation gain too.

GO FARTHER

While it's only a 0.2-mile trail, the walk out to Dumas Bay Sanctuary is quite pretty. Find the trailhead for this Federal Way Park on 44th Avenue SW, off of SR 509, about a mile northeast of Dash Point State Park.

21 West Hylebos Wetlands Park

DISTANCE:	1.4 miles of trails
ELEVATION GAIN:	Minimal
HIGH POINT:	225 feet
DIFFICULTY:	Easy
FITNESS:	Walkers, hikers
FAMILY-FRIENDLY:	Yes
DOG-FRIENDLY:	Prohibited
AMENITIES:	Privies, picnic tables, benches, interpretive signs
CONTACT/MAP:	City of Federal Way Parks and Recreation
GPS:	N 47 17.373, W 122 19.677
BEFORE YOU GO:	Park open dusk to dawn

GETTING THERE

Driving: From Tacoma, follow I-5 north to exit 142B. Then head west on S. 348th Street for 0.9 mile to the park and trailhead on your left. Overflow parking can be found at the South Federal Way Park and Ride, located just east of the park on S. 348th Street.

Transit: King County Metro line 182 stops at 6th Avenue S. and S. 348th Street.

Explore one of the last large peat bogs remaining in the South Puget Sound lowlands. The 120-acre West Hylebos Wetlands Park is an ecological gem located within minutes of shopping centers, busy arterials, and suburban housing tracts. But after you take to the trails here, which include a 1-mile boardwalk, you'll instantly feel like you're deep in the wilderness or back in time.

GET MOVING

A lot has changed in the Hylebos Creek drainage since Father Peter Francis Hylebos, a Belgian-born priest, came to Tacoma in 1880. Hylebos helped build churches, hospitals, and schools in the region. And while he was a big promoter for developing the region, he would probably be astounded today to see a booming city sprouting around these wetlands. But thanks to Ilene and Francis Marckx, a significant portion of the sensitive wetlands here have been protected.

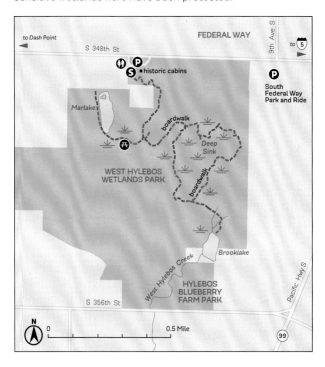

Back in 1955, long before there was a city of Federal Way, the Marckxs bought a large parcel of land that contained these wetlands. They soon realized the ecological value of the wetlands and grew concerned over the increasing development around them. They formed the Friends of the Hylebos and began looking for ways to preserve the land. In 1981, they donated 24.5 acres to the state to be used as a city park. Since then, various agencies and conservation groups have helped bring the preserve to 120 acres. Today it's owned and managed by Federal Way and is the pride of the city.

From the small parking lot, check out two historic structures before heading down the trail. Here find the 1883-built Barker Cabin (moved here in 1993), the oldest original building in Federal Way, and the 1889-built Denny Cabin, which was moved from Seattle to Federal Way and then to this spot in 1992. Now follow a wide gravel path winding through a small field and old orchard. In 0.2 mile, you'll reach a junction.

The trail to the right leads to a picnic area, then continues along the west shore of the small body of water known as Marlake. The path ends at private property in about 0.25 mile. It is a good trail for solitude and seeing birdlife. However, it can be quite muddy during the rainy season.

The trail to the left is the main attraction; follow it downhill, soon coming to the start of nearly a mile of well-built boardwalk. Soon the trail comes to a junction—here a loop can be made, and it matters not which direction you go. Branching off of the south end of the loop is a short spur boardwalk traveling over Hylebos Creek and ending at an observation platform at a body of water known as Brooklake.

The boardwalk loop is one of the most enjoyable and interesting hikes in the South Sound. Be sure to stop at all of the observation points and interpretive panels. Notice the large and abundant Sitka spruce growing in these wetlands—trees more commonly associated with the coast. And do check out the Deep Sink, a deep water-filled hole in the peat. In some

Boardwalk trail through West Hylebos Wetlands

places within this bog, the peat is more than 30 feet deep. Return to your start or take another walk along the boardwalk, a practice many visitors partake in.

GO FARTHER

Not too far to the south of West Hylebos Wetlands Park is the city of Fife's 15-acre Hylebos and Milgard Natural Areas. Here you can follow a 0.3-mile level trail along Hylebos Creek. Trailhead and parking can be found at the corner of 62nd Avenue E. and 8th Street E.

22 BPA Trail

DISTANCE:	3.6 miles one-way
ELEVATION GAIN:	Up to 900 feet
HIGH POINT:	420 feet
DIFFICULTY:	Easy to moderate
FITNESS:	Walkers, runners, bikers
FAMILY-FRIENDLY:	Yes, and jogger-stroller and wheelchair accessible
DOG-FRIENDLY:	On leash
AMENITIES:	Privies, benches
CONTACT/MAP:	City of Federal Way Parks and Recreation
GPS:	N 47 18.645, W 122 19.067
BEFORE YOU GO:	Trail and adjacent parks open dusk to dawn

GETTING THERE

Driving: From Tacoma, follow I-5 north to exit 142B. Then head west on S. 348th Street for 0.3 mile and turn right onto 16th Avenue S. Drive 0.5 mile and turn right (north) onto State Route 99 (Pacific Highway S). After 0.7 mile, turn left onto S. 330th Street. In 0.2 mile, the road bends to the right, becoming 13th Avenue S. Proceed another 0.1 mile and turn left into Celebration Park for trailhead and parking.

From Seattle follow I-5 south to Exit 143. Turn right onto S. 320th Street and drive 0.2 mile. Then turn left onto 23rd Ave S. (which becomes S. 324th Street) and continue 0.9 mile (crossing SR 99). Then turn left onto 13th Ave S. and drive 0.2 mile turning right into Celebration Park for trailhead and parking.

Transit: Pierce Transit line 500 and King County Metro Transit lines 903 and 182 stop near Celebration Park. Line 182 also stops near the south end of the BPA Trail, on SW 356th Street.

Run or walk this trail and get a great workout. Unlike rail trails that follow gentle grades, this paved path utilizes a powerline

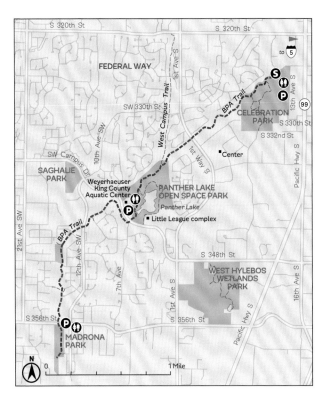

corridor across rolling hills. And despite the fact that towering high-tension wires accompany you the entire way, the trail traverses a couple of greenbelts and parks. And when the sun is out, you'll get some decent views of Mount Rainier and the Olympic Mountains to help get your mind off of all the ups and downs.

GET MOVING

The BPA Trail, which is named after the Bonneville Power Administration transmission line it follows, travels across a good chunk of Federal Way. It also weaves together a couple of the city's parks and greenbelts as well as the Weyerhaeuser King County Aquatic Center. There are several short spurs that branch off of it, connecting to abutting neighborhoods, including the 1-mile West Campus Trail. And at the trail's northeastern terminus in Celebration Park, you'll find nearly 2 more miles of trails to explore. It's easy to get in a long run or walk here. Of course most folks opt for shorter options, and you can access the BPA Trail from several points along the way.

From Celebration Park, reach the start of the BPA Trail by either walking the paved path that skirts the softball fields and parallels 13th Avenue S., or via one of two dirt paths that explores some of the woods in the 83.5-acre park. The BPA Trail starts at an elevation of 420 feet—its highest elevation. The trail heads out on a southwest course along a wide power-line swath. While high-tension wires dangle above, the swath is pretty green and lined with trees for much of its way.

BPA Trail's rolling terrain

The trail curves with the contours instead of just making a beeline. This makes the grades more manageable and the layout more aesthetically pleasing. The distance is marked on the trail in 0.1-mile increments.

The trail rolls on a generally downhill course, passing a couple of spurs leading to adjacent neighborhoods before coming to busy 1st Way S. at 1 mile. A pedestrian signal here allows for safe crossing. The trail then descends, coming to a junction with the West Campus Trail at 1.3 miles. This paved path leads north for 1 mile through a forested corridor, crossing a couple of streets before terminating at S. 320th Street (no parking).

From the junction with the West Campus Trail, the BPA Trail then enters the Panther Lake Open Space Park. Here two trails diverge. One is a short paved path to a viewpoint. Skip it. The viewpoint includes a bench often surrounded by trash and graffiti. The other trail is dirt and leads left. This trail is worth checking out. It's a newly constructed 1-mile interpretive path leading around the undeveloped lake to a parking area near the Little League complex on SW Campus Drive.

Continuing south, the BPA Trail skirts above the western shore of the lake. When foliage is thin, you can catch a few glimpses of it. At 1.9 miles, come to the King County Aquatic Center (parking available). Here the trail crosses busy SW Campus Drive (use the traffic light) and then starts to climb, paralleling SW Campus Drive. The trail climbs more than 150 feet, traveling through several neighborhoods and crossing several side roads. This section of trail is more suburban than the northern section.

The trail travels through a few pocket parks. There are also several spurs leading to neighboring streets. At 3.3 miles, the trail comes to SW 356th Street (parking available). Carefully cross the street to continue. The trail then traverses Madrona Park (parking and playground) and ends in 0.3 mile at the top of a bluff on the Federal Way–Tacoma border.

23 Milton Interurban Trail

DISTANCE:	2.5 miles one-way
ELEVATION GAIN:	225 feet
HIGH POINT:	250 feet
DIFFICULTY:	Easy
FITNESS:	Walkers, hikers, runners, bikers
FAMILY-FRIENDLY:	Yes, and jogger-stroller and wheelchair accessible
DOG-FRIENDLY:	On leash
AMENITIES:	Privy, benches, picnic tables
CONTACT/MAP:	City of Milton Parks and Recreation
GPS:	N 47 14.502, W 122 20.124
BEFORE YOU GO:	Open from dusk to dawn

GETTING THERE

Driving: From Tacoma, follow I-5 north to exit 137. Then turn right onto 54th Avenue E. and immediately turn left onto 20th Street

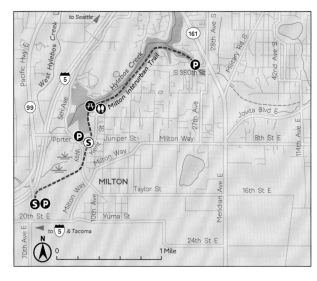

E. Continue for 1 mile and turn left onto 70th Avenue E. Then drive 0.2 mile and turn right into the trailhead parking area.

Transit: Pierce Transit line 501 stops at the corner of 20th Street E. and 70th Avenue E. Pierce Transit line 402 stops on State Route 161, not too far from the trail's eastern terminus.

Run or walk across wetlands and a pocket of farmland, watching for eagles, deer, and coyotes. Marvel at Mount Rainier rising over the Puyallup River Valley. Then traverse slopes of big cottonwoods and firs as you climb alongside a lush emerald ravine. And unlike the longer Interurban Trail that travels up the Green River Valley, this one actually has some elevation gain.

GET MOVING

This is a relatively new section of trail utilizing the old Puget Sound Electric Railway line. That interurban line once ran for 38 miles from Tacoma to Seattle, from 1902 until 1928. Elsewhere, most of the original line and converted trail runs across pretty flat terrain (see Trail 25)—but here in Milton, the trail climbs from the Puyallup River floodplain up a forested hill and along an emerald ravine. It is one of the prettier and more interesting sections of the old rail line turned trail.

From the parking lot, the trail follows a service road for a short distance before reaching the old rail line. The paved trail, which is marked in half-mile increments, then cuts across a plain, with farmland to the south and wetlands along Hylebos Creek to the north. Look for raptors, eagles, heron, deer, and the occasional coyote. And enjoy a stunning view of Mount Rainier hovering over the Puyallup Valley. Enjoy, too, the large cottonwoods lining the way.

At 0.6 mile, the trail crosses Porter Way and begins to climb. A quarter mile farther, it crosses Kent Street just a short distance from a park (parking and alternative start).

Autumn leaves collect on the trail.

The trail then takes on a wilder course as it begins to traverse a forested hillside over a ravine cradling Hylebos Creek. At 1.2 miles, the trail reaches a privy and picnic table. Stop for good creek views below. Notice the sandstone in the ravine attesting to unstable slopes. As the trail continues farther up the canyon, noise from nearby I-5 fades. The trail continues climbing and crosses a small creek before ending at 2.5 miles on S. 380th Street (street parking).

GO FARTHER

Definitely check out the eastern section of the Milton Interurban Trail in nearby Edgewood (parking and trailhead located on 114th Avenue E., just north of the intersection with Jovita Boulevard E.). Here you can run or walk along a new section of paved trail, passing through a wetland and skirting quiet neighborhoods, reaching Military Road S. (no parking). There are picnic tables and interpretive signs along the way. Unfortunately this stretch of trail is only 0.8 mile long, and until it's connected with the western section of the trail, it will remain lightly visited. There is no safe pedestrian connection between the trail sections.

Next page: *Sprawling fields in Flaming Geyser State Park*

AUBURN

Situated in the Green River Valley, where the White and Green Rivers once merged, Auburn was first settled by Euro-Americans in the 1850s. The area's rich soils helped nourish dairy, hops, and berry farms. By the late 1800s, railroads came through the area. The Interurban Railroad (now a trail; see Trail 25) allowed Auburn farmers to flourish by giving them direct access to Seattle and Tacoma markets. By the 1960s, the area's economy was becoming more industrial. Soon afterward, the city's close proximity to Puget Sound's major cities led to a retail and housing boom. Today Auburn is home to more than 80,000 people. The city has a good park system and a couple of good regional trails. And just to the east of the city are thousands of acres of preserved lands embracing the Green River. Here find patches of farmland, rich wildlife habitat, and miles of excellent trails.

24   White River Trail

DISTANCE:	2.25 miles one-way
ELEVATION GAIN:	80 feet
HIGH POINT:	160 feet
DIFFICULTY:	Easy
FITNESS:	Walkers, runners, bikers
FAMILY-FRIENDLY:	Yes, and jogger-stroller and wheelchair accessible
DOG-FRIENDLY:	On leash
AMENITIES:	Privies, benches, picnic tables and shelter, playground, campground
CONTACT/MAP:	City of Auburn Parks and Recreation
GPS:	N 47 16.760, W 122 11.747

GETTING THERE

Driving: From Tacoma, take I-5 north to exit 142A, and then follow State Route 18 east to Auburn for 4.3 miles, taking the exit for SR 164 (Auburn Way S.). Turn left onto SR 164 and

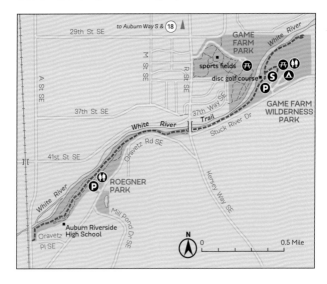

continue 0.9 mile. Then turn right onto Howard Road (just past 17th Street SE) and drive 0.2 mile. Next turn right onto R Street SE and proceed 1.2 miles. Upon crossing the White River, turn left onto Stuck River Drive and continue 0.6 mile. Then turn left into Game Farm Wilderness Park and continue to day-use parking and trailhead.

Walk along the tumbling glacier-fed White River between two lovely parks graced with big trees and pretty, natural settings. The paved White River Trail is a delight to walk or run any time of year. But winters can be particularly intriguing, when the rain-soaked river flows with a vengeance, and bald eagles roost in overhanging cottonwood branches.

GET MOVING

Locate the northern end of the trail in the Game Farm Wilderness Park. This park, along with the Game Farm Park (see Go Farther) across the river were once part of one of the state's nine game farms used to rear elk, pheasants, and other exotic game birds. Originally established in 1913 and expanded over the years, the Auburn game farm was shut down in 1978. The land was then turned over to Washington State Parks and became two beloved Auburn parks about a decade later. The two parks consist of 160 acres. The Game Farm Park across the river is fairly developed, while much of the Game Farm Wilderness Park's acreage has been left in a more natural state.

The two main draws to the wilderness park, aside from its trails and natural area, is its small campground (open year-round) and eighteen-hole disc golf course. The latter is the one you want to be aware of as you start your run or walk. The White River Trail cuts through this popular course, and you don't want to be reminded of that with a conk in the head. So be aware of flying objects when you first set out.

The trail eventually leaves the disc golf course and then runs alongside the White River, which is contained between

Family outing on the trail on a quiet winter day

two levees. The river here was once known as the Stuck River as it was an entirely different waterway than the White. The White River used to flow into the Green River not too far from this spot. But in 1906, the White River flooded and flowed entirely into the small Stuck River. The Stuck, in essence, became the final section (which flows into the Puyallup River) of the White River. Later attempts to redirect the river were met with resistance, leading to all kinds of disputes between various land owners and government agencies. In any case, the Stuck River no longer exists, but its name still exists in places around the region.

The trail follows the river downstream and southwest. It scoots under R Street SE and soon afterward enters the 21-acre Roegner Park (parking and restrooms). After a brief climb up a small forested bluff, the trail descends to cross an open grassy area. Several short soft-surface trails depart from the main path, allowing for short loops and diversions. Young walkers may want to stop at the park's playground, and all walkers may want to stop to admire some of the commissioned artwork on the park grounds. The trail continues through the park grounds before ending at A Street SE (no parking).

GO FARTHER
Across the river from the Game Farm Wilderness Park is the Game Farm Park. This popular park includes sports fields and courts, playgrounds, picnic shelters, and public artwork. You'll also find a level 1-mile paved loop trail here, ideal for a relaxing stroll.

25 Interurban Trail

DISTANCE:	15 miles one-way
ELEVATION GAIN:	Up to 100 feet
HIGH POINT:	80 feet
DIFFICULTY:	Easy
FITNESS:	Walkers, runners, bikers
FAMILY-FRIENDLY:	Yes, and paved trail is jogger-stroller and wheelchair accessible
DOG-FRIENDLY:	On leash
AMENITIES:	Restrooms, benches
CONTACT/MAP:	King County Parks
GPS:	N 47 15.906, W 122 15.593

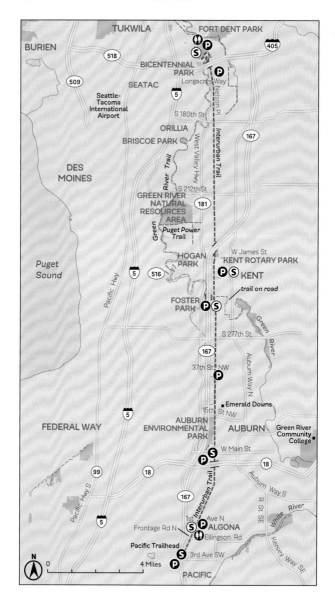

Bridge over the Green River

GETTING THERE

Driving to Pacific Trailhead: From Tacoma, follow State Route 167 (River Road) east to Puyallup and then continue on SR 167 (now the Valley Freeway) to the Ellingson Road exit in Pacific. Then turn right onto Ellingson Road and immediately turn right onto Frontage Road N. and drive 0.5 mile. Then turn left onto 3rd Avenue SW and drive 300 feet, reaching the trailhead and parking on your left.

Main Street Auburn Trailhead: From Tacoma, follow I-5 north to exit 142A and then follow State Route 18 east for 2.6 miles to the exit for West Valley Highway S. Turn left on West Valley Highway S. and drive 0.4 mile. Then turn right onto W. Main Street and drive 0.6 mile to the trailhead and parking on your right.

Other Trail Access Points (all have parking): Interurban Trailhead Park in Tukwila at Nelson Place and Longacres Way; Kent Rotary Basketball Court (near Kent-James Street Park and Ride in downtown Kent); Foster Park (S. 259th Street in Kent); Interurban Trailhead Park in Algona (1st Avenue N); and 37th Street NW in Auburn.

Transit: Interurban Trailhead Park in Algona: King County Metro 917. **15th Street Trail crossing in Auburn:** King County Metro 181, 917.

Run, walk, or bike part or all of this 15-mile paved path through the Kent Valley and never gain more than a few feet of elevation. Utilizing an old rail line and current utility right-of-way from Pacific to Tukwila, the Interurban Trail skirts scores of warehouses and distribution centers. But it also traverses hundreds of acres of wetlands as well. And on a clear day, Mount Rainier can be seen hovering over the surroundings from much of the trail.

GET MOVING

Popular with bicyclists, the Interurban Trail offers a safe traffic-free route through the heavily industrialized Green River Valley (Kent Valley). While it's not one of the region's most scenic rail trails, there are patches of wetlands along the way that add natural touches. Much of the trail's proximity to offices, commercial centers, and warehouses make it ideal for nearby workers to get a before- or after-work walk or run. The trail's southernmost stretch traverses neighborhoods, making it popular with families. And long-distance runners use this trail for training. When combined with the intersecting Green River Trail you can make a long lollipop loop.

The Interurban Trail follows nearly 15 miles of the old Puget Sound Electric Railway, a 38-mile interurban line that ran from Tacoma to Seattle from 1902 until 1928. A section in Milton (see Trail 23) and small section in Edgewood were converted to trail not too long ago. It would be great to see those stretches connected with the trail in Pacific someday soon.

From its southern terminus at a small park in Pacific, the trail heads northeast through a quiet neighborhood. The first half mile of the trail could use some repaving. Once the trail crosses busy Ellingson Road and enters Algona, in King County, though, it is in pretty decent shape. At 1 mile, it reaches the Interurban Trailhead Park (parking and restrooms) on 1st Avenue N.

The trail then passes businesses and comes up along the Union Pacific Railroad, which it will now parallel for most of the remaining way. It then enters Auburn, and at 2.3 miles crosses busy 15th Street SW (use the signal). It then makes a nearly straight shot north all the way to just south of the Green River. The trail ducks under SR 18 and reaches Auburn's W. Main Street (parking) at 3.2 miles. The trail then traverses lush expansive wetlands, proceeds under 15th Street NW, and passes the Emerald Downs Racetrack.

At 5.5 miles, the trail crosses 37th Street NW (parking). It then crosses 44th Street NW and shortly later darts under S. 277th Street, entering the city of Kent. The way then parallels a large railroad yard with lots of activity going on at its sidings. Next, the trail crosses the Green River and comes to a junction with the Green River Trail at Foster Park (parking) at 7.4 miles.

The trail then continues north, skirting downtown Kent and crossing several busy streets at surface level (use signals for safe crossings). It darts under SR 167 and then passes warehouses and light industries, drainage ditches, and small wetlands. At 12.4 miles, the trail passes beneath S. 180th and enters Tukwila. It then continues north, paralleling the busy West Valley Highway. The way skirts hotels and parking lots and makes a couple of surface-street crossings. At 13.9 miles, the trail leaves the old rail right-of-way and travels under I-405 and SW Grady Way. It then skirts around a hotel and amusement park, crosses the Green River, and terminates at the Green River Trail. From here it is 0.4 mile north on the Green River Trail to Fort Dent Park, where you'll find parking and restrooms.

GO FARTHER

From the Main Street Trailhead in Auburn, walk 0.3 mile west along Main Street to the Auburn Environmental Park's Boardwalk Trail. Here you can walk through this more than 200-acre wildlife-rich protected wetland on a 0.25-mile boardwalk, complete with interpretive signs and a birding tower. The trail ends on Western Street, where there is also parking. Kids and birders will absolutely love this park.

26 Green River College Trails

DISTANCE:	4 miles of trails
ELEVATION GAIN:	Up to 400 feet
HIGH POINT:	430 feet
DIFFICULTY:	Easy to moderate
FITNESS:	Walkers, runners, hikers
FAMILY-FRIENDLY:	Yes
DOG-FRIENDLY:	On leash
AMENITIES:	Benches
CONTACT/MAP:	Green River College Natural Resources Program
GPS:	N 47 18.660, W 122 10.754
BEFORE YOU GO:	College visitors can park in any unmarked parking spot, carpool parking spots after 10:30 AM, and staff parking spots after 5:00 PM (unless otherwise marked)

GETTING THERE

Driving: From Tacoma, take I-5 north to exit 142A and then follow State Route 18 east for 9 miles. Next take the exit for SE 304th Street and turn right. Now follow SE 304th Street (arterial becomes 132nd Avenue SE, then SE 312th Street) for 1.5 miles. Turn left onto 124th Avenue SE and drive 0.5 mile. Then turn left and enter the Green River College Campus and proceed to parking areas and trailheads.

Transit: King County Metro 181.

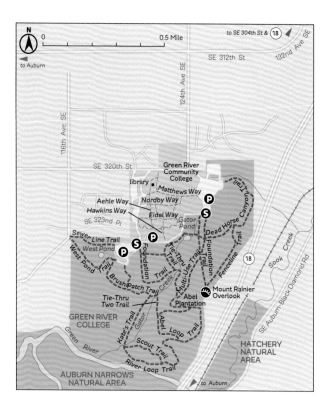

Green River College sits on a forested bluff high above the Green River. Surrounding the campus are more than 150 acres of forest. And branching out from the parking areas ringing the college buildings is a network of trails traversing that forest. Explore these trails for a good workout to the river or a gentle walk through groves of mature towering timber or for an inspiring view of Mount Rainier hovering above the valley.

GET MOVING

Developed and maintained by the college's Natural Resources Program, Green River College's trails are open to all. Natural

Green River along the River Loop Trail

Resources faculty and students can often be seen on these trails in some academic pursuit. And students and faculty from other departments regularly take to them for a walk between classes or a good run at the end of the day. You won't be alone hiking or running here—and you might learn a thing or two.

There are a few signed trailheads and signs along the way explaining projects and management operations. But overall, the trail system is poorly marked—so be sure to carry a map. Trails range from single track to paved paths to old roads. If you want fairly level, easy walking, stick to trails running from west to east along the campus hilltop. The West Pond Trail (which connects to a neighborhood west of campus), Interpretive Trail, Foundation Trail, and the Multi-Use Trail (open to bikes) all offer pretty easy grades and lots of loop options. An eastern section of the Foundation Trail is paved and leads to a stunning view (especially during early mornings and evenings) out to Mount Rainier. Don't get too excited over the Gator Pond—for it, like the West Pond, is pretty much a mudhole. But the forest ringing it is attractive, including some old-growth firs and cedars.

You can also add a loop to the Abel Plantation, which will give you a little elevation gain and loss. Just beyond the plantation are some interesting jumbled rock collections. If you want a good workout, take the River Loop Trail, which drops (and gains) about 350 feet on its way to the Green River. The west end of the loop (also known as Katie's Trail) is particularly steep, following a rib between two ravines. It makes a couple of bridged creek crossings and then follows along the river for a short stint. It would be a quiet spot if not for the nearby highway. The trail then more gradually ascends from the river to reach the Abel Loop. Be sure to check out the big cottonwoods along the way.

The Dead Horse Canyon Trail is another loop you can take. It includes a moderate elevation gain and loss. Utilizing various trails to make a grand loop will yield you between 2 and 2.5 miles, and you can easily double that mileage by adding smaller loops to the grand loop. If you're interested in a quick evening walk to see Rainier, it's about a half mile out and back.

27 Green River Natural Area

DISTANCE:	More than 7 miles of trails
ELEVATION GAIN:	Up to 650 feet
HIGH POINT:	500 feet
DIFFICULTY:	Easy to moderate
FITNESS:	Walkers, hikers, runners, bikers
FAMILY-FRIENDLY:	Yes, but be aware of equestrians
DOG-FRIENDLY:	On leash
AMENITIES:	Privies, benches, picnic tables
CONTACT/MAP:	King County Parks
GPS:	N 47 16.088, W 122 05.462

GETTING THERE

Driving: From Tacoma, take I-5 north to exit 142A and then follow State Route 18 east for 4.5 miles. Next take the exit for SR 164 (Auburn Way S) and turn left. Now follow SR 164 east for 5.7 miles and turn left onto SE 380th Street. Drive 0.2 mile and turn right onto 160th Place SE. Follow this road, which becomes SE 384th Street, for 1.8 miles. Then turn left onto 188th Avenue SE and drive 0.7 mile to O'Grady Trailhead and parking.

Located about midway between Auburn and Enumclaw is the sprawling Green River Natural Area. Within its 1200 acres, find riparian forests, forested hillsides, old farm pastures, oxbow ponds, wetlands, and several miles of frontage along the Green River. The area was established primarily to protect salmon habitat. But it's a recreational haven too, with more than 7 miles of well-built and uncrowded trails.

GET MOVING

The Green River Natural Area is composed of old farm-land and several former parks. O'Grady Park was one of the original protected tracts here and now serves as the natural area's most popular trailhead. Before this tract was acquired by King County, it was owned by the O'Grady family, who ran a large farm operation here, which included the cultivation of hops for making beer.

This area is extremely popular with equestrians, so be sure to yield to all horse traffic and to keep your dog under strict control. The Back Country Horsemen of Washington as well as the Washington Trails Association have done some excellent work here building and maintaining the area's large trail network. Trails are well marked and signed and there are wood-carved maps at many of the junctions.

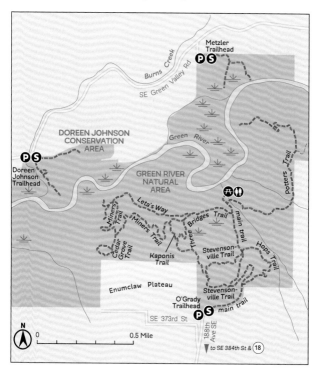

Gravel bar at the end of the Potters Trail

From the trailhead, an old (gated) service road now acts as the area's main trail and ties into many other trails. You're starting on the edge of the Enumclaw Plateau at an elevation of 500 feet. From here, the main trail descends 350 feet to the Green River. Remember to save some energy for the uphill return. You can head straight to the river on the main trail for a one-mile well-graded route and then return—or spend a couple of hours or all day exploring the area's other trails.

The main trail ends at an old pasture and apple orchard on a small bluff above the Green River, complete now with hitching post, picnic tables, benches, and privy. From here, you have lots of options for extending your hike or run. Potters Trail departs east, climbing 200 feet through an attractive mixed-conifer and deciduous forest. It crosses a small creek, traverses steep slopes, and then drops 200 feet to an old farm field. The trail then crosses the field to end at a large gravel bar on the river. This is one of the best spots in this area for accessing the river—and, come fall, for watching spawning salmon.

Departing west from the picnic area is the delightful Three Bridges Trail. Ironically you first come to an unbridged creek crossing before reaching the three bridges! This trail travels 0.7 mile, tying into other trails, including the 0.5-mile Stevensonville Trail, which will bring you back to the main trail. The Three Bridges Trail also leads to Leta's Way, which travels west for 0.5 mile along the river floodplain at the base of a bluff. It passes wetlands, channels, and groves of big cedars before terminating at the river near a channel.

You can return via the Miners Trail, which travels east for one mile on bluffs back to the Three Bridges Trail. If you want a diversion from this trail, you can take the 0.4-mile lollipop loop Cedar Grove Trail. This loop trail travels through a forested bluff that seems to have more maples than cedars.

A grand circuit around the O'Grady area will yield you just over 7 miles, enough to make for a good day hike or decent run. On the north side of the river and accessed from SE Green Valley Road are the Doreen Johnson and Metzler Trailheads. Here you can follow several short trails of a quarter or third mile to points along the river.

28 Flaming Geyser State Park

DISTANCE:	More than 5 miles of trails
ELEVATION GAIN:	Up to 250 feet
HIGH POINT:	420 feet
DIFFICULTY:	Easy to moderate
FITNESS:	Walkers, hikers, runners
FAMILY-FRIENDLY:	Yes
DOG-FRIENDLY:	On leash
AMENITIES:	Picnic tables and shelter, restrooms, water, interpretive displays
CONTACT/MAP:	Washington State Parks
GPS:	N 47 16.373, W 122 01.295
BEFORE YOU GO:	Discover Pass required

GETTING THERE

Driving: From Tacoma, take I-5 north to exit 142A and then follow State Route 18 east for 6.5 miles. Next take the exit for SE Auburn-Black Diamond Road. Turn right and then immediately turn right again onto SE Green Valley Road. Drive 8 miles and turn right into Flaming Geyser State Park. Continue 1.2 miles to parking and trailhead.

While this state park's namesake is now kaput, this 503-acre park still holds plenty of allure. Encompassing more than 3 miles of frontage on the Green River, sprawling fields, and quiet woodlots, Flaming Geyser State Park has been attracting picnickers, anglers, birders, and kayakers for decades. Hikers and runners have more than 5 miles of trails to explore. Beyond the trail that leads to a small bubbling geyser and an interpretive path, the park's trails are often pretty deserted.

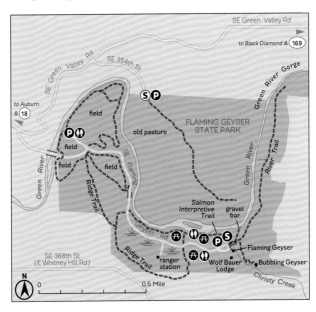

GET MOVING

Back in 1911, miners began drilling exploratory holes for coal here near Christy Creek. In one coal seam more than 1000 feet deep, the miners also hit pockets of methane and salt water. The methane and salt water seeped from the drill hole. Years later, coal-mine owner and entrepreneur Eugene Lawson ignited the methane. It blew as high as 25 feet, and salt water gushed from the hole as well. The flame continued to burn and became a marvel known as the flaming geyser. It spurred the development of a private park around it.

The park contained campsites, a river-fed swimming pool, and a fish hatchery. By the 1960s, however, the park went into bankruptcy, and the property was eyed for a housing development. Thankfully Washington State Parks acquired it. While

Green River from trail near picnic area

the flame diminished over the years, blowing a flame just a few inches high, visitors came to realize the real value of this park was its undeveloped frontage on the Green River.

From the trailhead at the end of the park road, check out steelhead imprint ponds. Then read the interpretive displays near the environmental learning lodge named for Wolf Bauer, a prominent German-American mountaineer and conservationist who died in 2016 at the age of 103. Now walk to the Flaming Geyser. It burns no more, but use imagination to picture it simultaneously spewing water and shooting a flame.

Walk over the bridge spanning cascading Christy Creek and take the short trail right to the Bubbling Geyser. This little trail steeply climbs, then drops via a set of steps to a forested hollow where the Bubbling Geyser gurgles in the creek. This geyser was also a coal test pit that hit methane. But here the methane is broken down by microbes and, when it comes into contact with the calcium in the creek, it produces calcium carbonate, creating the bubbling you see before you.

Once you have marveled at the park's geyser history, hit some of the trails traversing this swath of greenery along the Green River. From the Bubbling Geyser Trail junction near the bridge, two other trails diverge. The one closest to the creek leads a short way to the Green River. The other, the River Trail, climbs along some steep slopes, then descends to travel along a narrow floodplain (muddy at times) graced with thickets of salmonberries, big maples and cedars, and a few Sitka spruces. It passes some access points to the river before eventually petering out at 0.8 mile at the mouth of the Green River Gorge.

Back at the bridge, you can follow a paved path west, the wheelchair-accessible Salmon Interpretive Trail, which travels along a channel (look for spawning salmon in season) and through the picnic area. You can then continue through the open picnic area and pick up more riverside trail for a short while, eventually coming to the park road.

Across from the picnic area, about 0.25 mile west of the River Trailhead, is the Ridge Trail. This trail is great for solitude. Starting from a gated old service road, it traverses a wetland teeming with amphibians, birds—and at times mosquitoes— before beginning to climb 200 feet or so up wooded slopes and settling on a forested bench above the floodplain. The way passes through a maple arch and a grove of attractive cedars before descending and terminating in a large field in about a mile. From here you can retrace your steps or follow a trail right through the field to the road and then walk the riverside trail back to your start.

You can also take a trail that leads left to a field (occasionally sharing this trail with equestrians) and then pass the attractive park entrance bridge and continue on a trail through another field. This field is often used by model airplane aficionados, so you might have some distractions. The trail loops around the field, but take the path that splits left from it and drops into forest and hugs the river before returning to the field. This complete field foray from the Ridge Trail junction is about 1.3 miles. You can then walk alongside the park road a short distance to pick up the riverside trail. A complete loop involving the fields, riverside trail, and Ridge Trail is about 3.2 miles. Add an out-and-back on the River Trail and you're looking at close to 5 miles.

GO FARTHER

On the north side of the river, you can follow an old road turned trail and explore an old pasture, now part of the park. Reach the trailhead via SE 354th Street. Be sure to respect adjacent private property.

Next page: *Tunnel of greenery along the Route 66 Trail*

MAPLE VALLEY, BLACK DIAMOND, AND ENUMCLAW

Once sleepy towns on the edge of greater Pugetopolis, these three communities have seen tremendous growth in the last quarter century. Of the three, Enumclaw, situated on a fertile plateau that was formed by an old mudflow above the White and Green Rivers, has retained more of its rural past. A gateway to Mount Rainier National Park, Enumclaw is still surrounded by farms; this small city of 12,000 has also retained the character of its early twentieth-century downtown.

Black Diamond (population 5000) was born as a company coal town. Italian and Welsh immigrants were the first of several groups to settle in the town to work the mines. Many other ethnic groups followed, helping to give this city a diverse population and colorful history. The coal industry eventually declined, but there are still some active mining claims in the area. King County Parks is acquiring large tracts of former Palmer Coking Coal Company lands and converting them to parks and open space. Large new housing developments have begun, too.

Maple Valley's origins are in the timber industry as well as the coal industry. The area's large lakes gave birth to a couple of resorts. By the 1980s, suburbanization was in full swing, and several of the city's surrounding tree farms were converted into housing developments. This once quiet corner of King County is now home to more than 30,000. Fortunately, King County Parks is preserving large swaths of forests as open space and parks, and the city is building a trail system that is rapidly becoming one of the region's largest.

29 Cedar River Trail

DISTANCE:	5.7 miles one-way
ELEVATION GAIN:	Up to 550 feet
HIGH POINT:	550 feet
DIFFICULTY:	Easy
FITNESS:	Walkers, hikers, runners, bikers
FAMILY-FRIENDLY:	Yes, and jogger-stroller friendly
DOG-FRIENDLY:	On leash
AMENITIES:	Restrooms, picnic shelters, benches
CONTACT/MAP:	King County Parks
GPS:	N 47 22.519, W 121 58.302

GETTING THERE

Driving: From Tacoma, follow I-5 north to exit 142A and then follow State Route 18 east for 18 miles to the exit for 244th Avenue SE. Turn right onto 244th Avenue SE and drive 0.5 mile. Next turn left onto SE 216th Street and proceed for 2 miles. Then turn right onto 276th Avenue SE (Issaquah-Ravensdale Road), which becomes Landsburg Road SE, and drive 2.4 miles to trailhead and parking on your right.

Trail can also be accessed from the following parks or locations (all have parking): at its western terminus at Nishwaki Lane in downtown Renton; Cedar River Park off of Houser Way N; Riverview Park (off of SR 169); Ron Regis Park (access 149th SE from SR 169); and the parking area off of SR 169 near the SR 18 overpass just north of Maple Valley.

Transit: King County Metro routes 143 and 907 access the trail at various stops along SR 169 (Maple Valley Highway).

Walk or run from the Landsburg Headworks Historic District, at the boundary of Seattle's Cedar River Watershed, along the river to Lake Washington. Although a good stretch of the Cedar River Trail's 17.3 miles are paved and more appealing to cyclists than pedestrians, the easternmost 5.7 miles

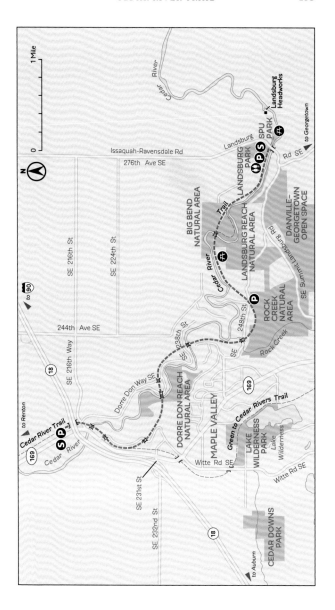

described here traverse a quiet rural landscape. Walk or run along the rippling river through a series of parks and greenbelts—and marvel at it from above on some old trestle bridges.

GET MOVING

The Cedar River Trail begins just downriver from the City of Seattle's Landsburg Headworks. It was here that in 1901, water began being diverted from the river into an aqueduct to supply Seattle with much of its water needs. Seattle Public Utilities maintains a small park just across Landsburg Road SE. Carefully cross the road and check it out. Here you'll find interpretive displays on the historic headworks district as well as a picnic and wading area and a fish ladder. This is a great spot for observing salmon.

The wide unpaved trail—a former line of the Chicago, Milwaukee, Saint Paul, and Pacific Railroad—heads west, paralleling the river. The trail is well shaded with plenty of large big-leaf maples along the way. The river churns and ripples, creating a delightful ambience. Pass an inviting picnic table before coming to a bird-rich oxbow pond on your right.

The trail then crosses a deep cut (one of the few on this trail) as the way leaves the river. Here the river makes a big bend, and the trail enters King County's Big Bend Natural Area. This area, along with the nearby Landsburg Reach Natural Area (which the trail briefly passes through), contains 120 acres of natural habitat along both sides of the river. Several informal trails traverse the properties, leading to fishing spots and gravel bars favored by dog owners and locals seeking heat relief in the summer.

At 1.2 miles, the trail crosses the river on an attractive old truss bridge. It then crosses another cut and passes by a picnic table set on a bluff above the river. From here the trail runs alongside the river once again until the river departs for another bend. At 2.1 miles, the trail crosses SE 248th Street

Truss bridge spanning the Cedar River

(parking available) and then traverses a wooded area before crossing SE 248th Street once again—this time on a bridge, at 2.6 miles. The way now passes through woods and wetlands, coming to another attractive truss bridge spanning high above the river at 3.2 miles. This is a good spot to turn around.

The trail continues through woods and by rural homes, coming to another truss crossing at 4 miles. From here it pulls away from the river and reaches a junction with the Green to Cedar Rivers Trail (see Trail 30) at 4.8 miles. The trail then becomes paved and crosses the river on a truss and ducks under SE 216th Way and SR 18 before reaching a parking area along SR 169 at 5.7 miles. From here the trail parallels SR 169 for most of its remaining 11.6 miles, ending at Lake Washington in Renton.

30 Green to Cedar Rivers Trail

DISTANCE:	3.3 miles one-way
ELEVATION GAIN:	Up to 250 feet
HIGH POINT:	550 feet
DIFFICULTY:	Easy
FITNESS:	Walkers, hikers, runners, bikers
FAMILY-FRIENDLY:	Yes, and jogger-stroller friendly
DOG-FRIENDLY:	On leash
AMENITIES:	Restrooms, drinking water, picnic shelters, benches, playground, ball fields, beach, arboretum at Lake Wilderness Park
CONTACT/MAP:	King County Parks
GPS:	N 47 22.742, W 122 02.335
BEFORE YOU GO:	Lake Wilderness Park open 7:00 AM to dusk

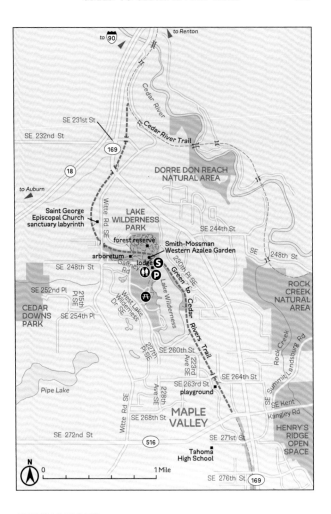

GETTING THERE

Driving: From Tacoma, follow I-5 north to exit 142A and then follow State Route 18 east for 15.8 miles. Next take the exit for SE 231st Street in Maple Valley. Turn right and then immediately turn right again onto SR 169 and follow for 0.3 mile. Then

Trail along Lake Wilderness

turn right onto Witte Road SE and drive for 0.8 mile to a traffic circle. Exit the circle onto SE 248th Street and drive east 0.3 mile. Then bear right onto Gaffney Road and continue 0.2 mile to parking and trailhead in Lake Wilderness Park.

From Seattle, follow I-5 to I-405 and take exit 4 in Renton. Then drive SR 169 south for 11.3 miles turning right onto Witte Road SE. Then follow directions above from Witte Road SE.

Transit: King County Metro route 168 stops at trailhead on State Route 516 (SE Kent Kangley Road).

Walk or run along this delightful rail trail, passing through quiet neighborhoods and a grove of towering timber and along a shimmering lake. The Green to Cedar Rivers Trail will one day connect the Cedar River Trail with Flaming Geyser State Park (see Trail 28). But for now, be content with 3.3 miles of family-friendly trail that pass beneath busy arterials and through lovely Lake Wilderness Park, which is home to more trails, a children's discovery forest, an intriguing arboretum, and stunning views of Mount Rainier.

GET MOVING

From the parking areas, walk northeast past the Lake Wilderness Lodge (home to Maple Valley's Park and Recreation Department and a programs center) and enter the 42-acre Lake Wilderness Arboretum (see Go Farther) before coming to the Green to Cedar Rivers Trail in 0.1 mile. Now decide whether you want to explore north or south. The latter is more scenic and therefore more popular. Either direction makes for a great walking or running route.

Northbound you'll pass feeder trails to both the arboretum on your left, and Lake Wilderness Park's Forest Reserve trail system on your right (see Go Farther). The trail is wide, smooth, and well graded. King County Parks plans to pave it soon, no doubt making it a more popular destination for cyclists. After 0.3 mile, the trail leaves the park, skirts a neighborhood, and ducks under Witte Road at 0.5 mile. Here a ramp and stairway lead to the road above for trailhead access (no parking).

The trail then soon comes upon Saint George Episcopal Church's sanctuary. Feel free to walk the sanctuary's labyrinth (open 7:00 AM to dusk). Walking a labyrinth involves following circular pathways to a center. It is an ancient form of meditative prayer. Once you have found your inner peace, continue on the trail.

Under a shady canopy, the path slowly descends, coming to the SR 169 underpass at 1.2 miles. The trail then skirts some businesses—side trails leading to a few of them. At 1.5 miles, the trail travels through the SE 231st Street underpass. Soon afterward, it makes a quick descent and terminates at 1.8 miles at the Cedar River Trail (see Trail 29).

South from Lake Wilderness Park, the trail passes a couple of side trails before reaching the shoreline of Lake Wilderness.

While no longer a wilderness—with homes crowding its shores in spots—it's still a pretty body of water. The trail then slowly ascends a slope of towering timber above the lake. It passes a side trail that leads left to 230th Place SE before traversing a private park and skirting some homes. Benches along the way invite a break. The way then passes a couple more side trails and a playground near SE 263rd Street at 1.1 miles. Then it travels between neighborhoods and commercial centers before coming to SR 516 at 1.5 miles.

GO FARTHER

The trail continues south (use caution crossing SR 516) as a narrow paved path, traveling behind shopping plazas and reaching SE 271st Place in 0.25 mile. It then continues as a rougher corridor paralleling SR 169 and reaching an active rail line just before Black Diamond Open Space (see Trail 33) at 1.2 miles. King County Parks has plans to eventually upgrade this stretch and continue it all the way to the Green River at Flaming Geyser State Park (see Trail 28).

Lake Wilderness Park's arboretum contains a couple of miles of well-maintained, interconnected, quiet wooded trails that connect with the Green to Cedar Rivers Trail. The trails are named for trees but are mostly unsigned (map available online from the arboretum). Except for the Hemlock and Oak Trails, they are pretty level. Walk along the lake, too, for a satisfying view of Mount Rainier rising above it.

South of the Green to Cedar Rivers Trail within the arboretum are some decent, albeit short paths also worth checking out. The Main Loop Trail is good for strolling, while the other paths require some stopping, observing, and learning. The Tribal Life Trail explains native plants usage by Native peoples. And the Smith-Mossman Western Azalea Garden contains one of the largest collections of this showy member of the heath family. Plan to visit during the spring bloom.

31 Cedar Downs and Cedar Creek Parks

DISTANCE:	About 2.6 miles of trails
ELEVATION GAIN:	Up to 300 feet
HIGH POINT:	600 feet
DIFFICULTY:	Easy to moderate
FITNESS:	Walkers, hikers, runners, bikers
FAMILY-FRIENDLY:	Yes
DOG-FRIENDLY:	On leash
AMENITIES:	Benches
CONTACT/MAP:	King County Parks and City of Covington; map available from Friends of Cedar Creek
GPS:	N 47 22.543, W 122 03.521
BEFORE YOU GO:	Limited parking; do not block driveways

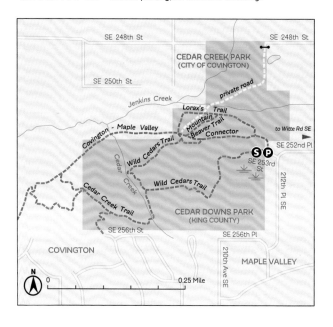

GETTING THERE

Driving: From Tacoma, follow I-5 north to exit 142A and then follow State Route 18 east for 15.8 miles. Next take the exit for SE 231st Street in Maple Valley. Turn right and then immediately turn right again onto SR 169 and follow for 0.3 mile. Then turn right onto Witte Road SE and drive for 1.2 miles. Next turn right onto SE 254th Place and proceed for 0.3 mile. Then turn right onto 215th Place SE. Continue for 0.1 mile, bearing left onto SE 252nd Place. Drive 0.2 mile and turn right onto SE 253rd Street and come to the trailhead within 200 feet. Park on the right side of road.

From Seattle, follow I-5 to I-405 and take exit 4 in Renton. Then drive SR 169 south for 11.3 miles turning right onto Witte Road SE. Then follow directions above from Witte Road SE.

Take a quiet hike among groves of big cedars, mossy maples, and a scattering of scaly-barked Sitka spruce trees in a quiet little wedge of nature. Straddling the Maple Valley–Covington city line and surrounded by subdivisions, these two adjacent parks preserve a piece of South King County that is rapidly fading away: intact mature woodlands. Take to more than 2.5 miles of trails exploring forested hillsides, a deep ravine, a rich wetland, and a salmon-spawning creek.

GET MOVING

Surrounded by suburbanization, much of this 127-acre protected forestland was once part of a Department of Natural Resources tract managed for timber production. Fortunately the last time the tract was logged was in 1930s, meaning there are some large mature trees gracing the property. And as the parks' names denote—you can expect many of those trees to be western red cedars.

From the small parking lot, head out to explore. The trail system here is confusing. While the Friends of Cedar Creek have published a map, some of the trails they show on it don't yet exist. And other paths not shown on the map, mainly bootleg trails built by local mountain bikers, further make navigating here befuddling at times. No worries as the area is not that large. King County Parks has signed most of the official trails in the county park, making things a little easier.

An old dirt road traverses the property from east to west and will someday be part of a trail that connects Covington and Maple Valley. Several of the parks' trails tie into it,

Big cedar in Cedar Creek Park

allowing for some good loops to be made. The terrain is rolling, so expect a little elevation gain. The Wild Cedars Trail is one of the more attractive trails in the complex. Follow it for 0.7 mile to the Covington–Maple Valley Connector Trail and then follow that trail 0.3 mile east back to the trailhead for a 1-mile loop with about 180 feet of elevation gain.

The Cedar Creek Trail leaves the Wild Cedars Trail about midway and ties into the Covington–Maple Valley Connector Trail in 0.4 mile, allowing for a longer loop of about 1.8 miles. If you follow the connector west, you'll soon leave park land and come to a natural gas right-of-way. Cedar Creek, which is a trickle much of the year, flows through a steep ravine to connect with the much longer and salmon-important Jenkins Creek. You can get some close-up views of this creek by following the Lorax's Trail, which is also an old road. The wetlands surrounding this creek provide excellent habitat for myriad wildlife—and at times, mosquitoes. Hopefully, though, you may spot herons, deer, or perhaps a coyote instead.

32 Danville-Georgetown Open Space

DISTANCE:	More than 25 miles of trails
ELEVATION GAIN:	Up to 300 feet
HIGH POINT:	800 feet
DIFFICULTY:	Easy to moderate
FITNESS:	Walkers, hikers, runners
FAMILY-FRIENDLY:	Yes, but trails are heavily used by equestrians, so be aware
DOG-FRIENDLY:	On leash and under strict control
CONTACT/MAP:	King County Parks
GPS:	N 47 22.235, W 122 00.390
BEFORE YOU GO:	Trails are confusing; print or upload map before going

GETTING THERE

Driving: From Tacoma, follow I-5 north to exit 142A and then follow State Route 18 east for 11.2 miles to the exit for SR 516 in Covington. Turn right and follow SR 516 (SE 272nd Street, which becomes SE Kent Kangley Road) for 4.7 miles to a junction with SR 169. Continue east on SE Kent Kangley Road for 0.2 mile. Then turn left onto SE Summit Landsburg Road and drive 1 mile to the trailhead on your left.

Explore miles and miles of lightly traveled trails through old woodlots that are slowly being restored to a more natural state. Maintained by the Back Country Horsemen of Washington's Tahoma Chapter, these trails are primarily used by equestrians. But hikers and runners are invited to use them too. Set out on a short and easy stroll or an all-day romp

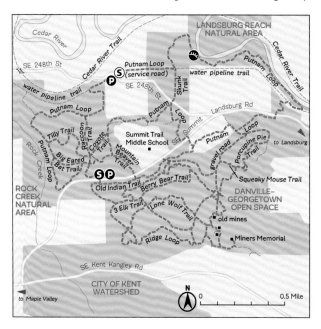

traveling through quiet forest groves, along the rippling Cedar River, or to a hillside with old mine sites.

GET MOVING

While these trails are open to bikes too, bikes are better suited for the nearby Henry's Ridge and Black Diamond Open Space areas (see Trail 33). Horse use is the primary recreation mode of many of the trails within Danville-Georgetown, so be prepared to yield to the big beasties (and talk in a calming voice when approached by them) and expect a few "road apples" in the trail. The trails south of Summit Landsburg Road tend to see lighter horse use.

Danville-Georgetown Open Space comprises 334 acres of formerly working forestland. The area was named for the old Danville railroad line that once traveled through the site and for the old mining town of Georgetown. This open space area is now being managed for recreation, wildlife management, and forest management.

Bordering Danville-Georgetown are several other large protected tracts of land: King County's 143-acre Rock Creek Natural Area and 24-acre Landsburg Reach Natural Area, and the City of Kent's 315-acre watershed forest. Connecting trails travel through the two natural areas (the watershed is closed to the public) as well as some adjacent private land and school property. The trail system is complex, but it's poorly signed in places. It's easy to get disoriented, and there are several old roads in the complex not on maps that can further add to confusion. Stick to signed trails, and as you learn the system, branch out. Always respect any closures and posted private property.

One of the more popular and well-trodden trails is the Putnam Loop. This trail travels along a good portion of the periphery of the northern section of the open space and utilizes part of the wide water pipeline trail (a service road). It's fairly level except for a section along a high bluff on the Cedar

Tunnel of vine maples along the Putnam Loop Trail

River and where it crosses the Summit Landsburg Road to the east. The trail then crosses the road again and circles around Summit Trail Middle School to complete the loop. It's around 4.5 miles and connects to many other trails in the open space. The section along the river is particularly pretty, with bluff-top river views (use caution) and a section of overhanging vine maple forest.

Trails south of the Summit Landsburg Road traverse a small hill. These trails tend to have smoother tread than the ones frequented by horses. Here you can add a little elevation gain to your hike or run. Put together some loops on whimsically

FRANKLIN, WASHINGTON— A GHOST TOWN

Coal mining was one of the region's largest industries from the 1860s until the early twentieth century. By the end of World War I in 1918, more than four million tons of coal had been mined in Washington. Financed largely by California and East Coast investors, local coal was used to power the growing railroads both here and in California, as well as to heat and power local homes and industries. While oil, gas, and hydroelectric energy (as well as environmental and labor concerns) would ultimately help lead to coal's demise in Puget Sound (and throughout the state), coal was mined in the region until the 1970s. The last mine in the area was closed in Ravensdale in 1974.

Many of the outlying towns and communities covered in this book were founded around the coal industry: Black Diamond, Carbonado, Ravensdale, and Wilkeson among them. Some of the largest coal mines in the region were located in the town of Franklin, which no longer exists. A ghost town with an intriguing history, it can now be reached by trail.

Franklin was established in the 1880s as a company town. It was heavily settled by English, Irish, Italian, Scottish, and Welsh immigrants. Like other coal-mining communities in the area, the railroad was extended to it so that coal could be readily transported for export to California. In 1891, labor recruiters brought African Americans from Southern and Midwestern states to be used as strikebreakers (unbeknownst to them), causing tensions with the immigrant workforce and resulting in a riot and the death of two workers.

named trails: Berry Bear, 3 Elk, Old Indian, Lone Wolf, Squeaky Mouse, and Porcupine Pie. And combined with the Putnam Loop, you can easily put together a hike or run of more than 7 miles that travels around the open space's periphery.

To the east of this section, trails continue on old coal-mining lands. Use caution here and never enter the old mining depressions. A trail off of Ridge Loop leads to Miners Memorial, a sobering reminder of the harsh and often dangerous working conditions that coal miners faced. Here, in 1955, four coal miners lost their lives when the Landsburg mine no. 1 caved in on them.

On August 24, 1894, one of the state's worst mine disasters occurred here when a fire broke out (later determined to be maliciously set) in one of the mines causing the death of thirty-seven miners. By the early twentieth century, with coal demand in decline, the town began to wane. By 1919, the last mine in town closed and most of the residents left.

After World War II and up until 1971, the Palmer Coking Coal Company resumed mining around the town site. Today all that remains, where once homes, saloons, a school, hotel, and other buildings stood, are foundations and the cemetery. You can easily hike to the Franklin site by following an old railroad grade. You'll pass a coal cart, sealed mine, powerhouse foundation, and penstock before coming to the cemetery at 1.2 miles from the trailhead.

While the town site is located on state parks property, the start of the hike and parking area is privately owned. A fee is charged (currently $5 a car; bring cash). Respect all rules and posted property. Access can be revoked at any time. To reach the trailhead, drive east from Black Diamond on Lawson Street (which becomes the Franklin Howard Road and then SE Green River Gorge Road) for 3.3 miles to a parking area on your right just before the bridge over the Green River. Afterward, consider checking out the scenic trails (fee charged) in the eclectic Green River Gorge Resort located just over the bridge.

33 Black Diamond and Henry's Ridge Open Spaces

DISTANCE:	More than 15 miles of trails
ELEVATION GAIN:	Up to 300 feet
HIGH POINT:	800 feet
DIFFICULTY:	Easy to moderate
FITNESS:	Walkers, hikers, runners, bikers
FAMILY-FRIENDLY:	Yes, but many trails are heavily used by mountain bikers, so be aware
DOG-FRIENDLY:	On leash; be aware of bikes
AMENITIES:	Privies, picnic tables, map kiosks
CONTACT/MAP:	King County Parks
GPS:	N 47 20.159, W 122 00.765
BEFORE YOU GO:	Mountain bikes have right-of-way; plan hikes and runs for quieter weekdays

GETTING THERE

Driving: From Tacoma, follow I-5 north to exit 142A and then follow State Route 18 east for 11.2 miles to the exit for SR 516 in Covington. Turn right and follow SR 516 (SE 272nd Street, which becomes SE Kent Kangley Road) for 4.7 miles to junction with SR 169. Then turn right and drive 1.8 miles to parking and trailhead on your left (additional parking on your right).

Primarily a mountain bike park, there are a few trails within this sprawling greenbelt between Maple Valley, Black Diamond, and Ravensdale suitable for hiking and trail running. The best pedestrian routes here follow Ravensdale Creek to Ravensdale Lake. Travel alongside a wildlife-rich wetland and through a couple of impressive groves of mature trees.

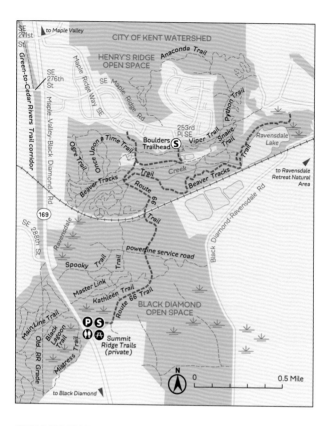

GET MOVING

Consisting of more than 1200 acres in three units, the Black Diamond Open Space and adjacent Henry's Ridge Open Space were set aside to mitigate new developments in the area. Much of the Black Diamond Open Space section consists of former woodlots. The forest here is young and scrappy except for along Ravensdale Creek, where older trees can be found. The Henry's Ridge Open Space wraps around a housing development.

Old roads on the property now make good multiuse trails. Almost all of the trails here were constructed by mountain bike groups. These trails are heavily curved (flowy), and many appear as spaghetti heaps on the map. Mountain bikers have the right-of-way on these trails, and running or walking them is generally not a good idea except during low-use times—and even then, you need to be aware of fast bikes on trails with poor long-range visibility.

From the trailhead, you'll want to take the Route 66 Trail, which is an old road. This wide trail is generally shunned by bikers in favor of the adjacent flowy trails. In 0.1 mile, bear left at a junction. The trail right heads to the Summit Ridge Trail System, a church-owned property developed for mountain bike use.

The Route 66 Trail continues north on a fairly level route through scrappy forest. After passing several trail junctions and crossing a powerline swath, the trail reaches an active railroad at 0.9 mile. Use caution crossing it and then continue on the Route 66 Trail through older, more attractive forest. The trail passes more bike trails before crossing Ravensdale Creek at 1.2 miles and coming shortly afterward to a junction with the Beaver Tracks Trail.

From here the Route 66 Trail begins to climb, soon coming to a storm retention pond in a clearing. At a junction with another road-turned-trail, the Route 66 Trail continues left, ending at a housing development on Maple Ridge Way SE at 1.5 miles. The other road-trail travels east for 0.25 mile to a pair of often-dry old ponds left over from when the land was used for industrial purposes. The trail then bends north and reaches in 0.1 mile the Boulders Trailhead (no parking) on 253rd Place SE.

The prime walk in this complex is to follow the Beaver Tracks Trail east from Route 66. Not as heavily biked as other trails here, this path is a real delight to walk. It meanders alongside Ravensdale Creek, passing a large bird-rich wetland. It then traverses young forest before reaching Ravensdale Lake. The path can then be followed a little farther on an

Storm retention pond along the Route 66 Trail

up-and-down course to big maples and a beautiful grove of old-growth firs and cedars. At about 1.2 miles from the Route 66 junction, the route peters out. It does continue a little farther, but it's often choked with blackberries and not worth sacrificing skin and cloth to go farther. On the return, it's possible to connect via a short trail with the road-trail that skirts the old industrial ponds for a loop back to the Route 66 Trail.

There is another mishmash of trails accessible from the parking lot and trailhead on the west side of SR 169. These too are primarily the domain of mountain bikers. You can follow an old railroad grade through the property. It makes for a good walk, and it will someday be part of the Green to Cedar Rivers Trail.

GO FARTHER

Not too far east is King County's 145-acre Ravensdale Retreat Natural Area. From the parking lot and trailhead in Ravensdale Park on SE Ravensdale Way, you can follow a quiet, fairly level trail east through young forest along Rock Creek for about a mile. The path then crosses a road and connects to a series of short loops around a small pond.

34 Lake Sawyer Regional Park

DISTANCE:	2 miles roundtrip
ELEVATION GAIN:	50 feet
HIGH POINT:	550 feet
DIFFICULTY:	Easy
FITNESS:	Walkers, hikers, runners
FAMILY-FRIENDLY:	Yes, and jogger-stroller friendly
DOG-FRIENDLY:	On leash
AMENITIES:	Privy, picnic tables, benches, interpretive signs
CONTACT/MAP:	City of Black Diamond Parks (no map online)
GPS:	N 47 19.270, W 122 02.253

GETTING THERE

Driving: From Tacoma, follow I-5 north to exit 142A and then follow State Route 18 east for 6.3 miles and take the exit for SE Auburn-Black Diamond Road. Turn right and after 0.3 mile, turn right onto SE Lake Holm Road. Follow this road east for 4.5 miles. Turn right onto SE Auburn-Black Diamond Road and continue 3.2 miles, bearing left onto Lake Sawyer Road SE. Drive 0.7 mile and turn right into the parking lot for the trailhead.

Hike a new trail in a new park through attractive forest to an undeveloped cove on Lake Sawyer, one of the largest lakes in King County. Wander by a wildlife-rich wetland and check out what lives along Ravensdale Creek as well. This 150-acre park is in an area exploding with new homes. As the area continues to grow and the park is upgraded with more trails and facilities, it's sure to become a popular draw.

GET MOVING

King County acquired this parcel with its rare tract of undeveloped shoreline on Lake Sawyer (6000 feet of shoreline) from the Palmer Coking Coal Company back in 1998. The county has

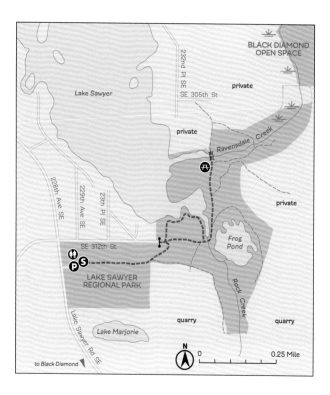

since turned it over to the City of Black Diamond, which only recently developed a parking lot and trail to the lakeshore. Future plans call for developing athletic fields. This will surely change the current, more sedate atmosphere of the park.

From the trailhead, walk the wide gravel trail through thick forest. At 0.25 mile, head left at a junction and reach a gated road at 0.4 mile (the old entrance) and a clearing by the lake. If you want to explore the lakeshore, head straight on a grassy lane framed by towering trees. You can walk a good 0.2 mile or so along the shore here. Through much of the year, it is a tranquil spot. But come summer, the jarring whine of jet skiers aimlessly spinning around in circles can be an annoyance.

Ravensdale Creek

To continue exploring, head right on the old road, which now serves as a trail. It will eventually become part of the Lake Sawyer Trail, which will connect this park to the Green to Cedar Rivers Trail (Trail 30) in the Black Diamond Open Space (Trail 33). The trail passes a few interpretive signs along the grassy, wildlife-rich wetland (a former cove since severed from the lake) locally known as Frog Pond. An unmaintained trail (brushy with thorny plants) runs along its eastern shore.

The main trail ends at 0.8 mile at a picnic area where Ravensdale Creek flows into Lake Sawyer. It's a pretty spot that is usually occupied by various waterfowl species. The old road continues north but enters posted private property. There are also several rough user-built trails leading right from the main trail that ultimately connect with trails in the Black Diamond Open Space area. Some cross private property, and they can be confusing to follow. Hopefully as this park develops, the trail system here will be upgraded as well, built to good standards and well posted. There is great potential for an excellent trail network to be here someday.

35 Kanaskat-Palmer State Park

DISTANCE:	2.5-mile loop
ELEVATION GAIN:	175 feet
HIGH POINT:	850 feet
DIFFICULTY:	Easy
FITNESS:	Hikers
FAMILY-FRIENDLY:	Yes
DOG-FRIENDLY:	On leash
AMENITIES:	Privies, benches, water, campground, picnic tables and shelters
CONTACT/MAP:	Washington State Parks
GPS:	N 47 19.320, W 121 54.427
BEFORE YOU GO:	Discover Pass required; park open 8:00 AM to dusk

GETTING THERE

Driving: From Tacoma, follow I-5 north to exit 142A and then follow State Route 18 east for 11.2 miles to the exit for SR 516 in Covington. Turn right and follow SR 516 (SE 272nd Street, which becomes SE Kent Kangley Road) for 4.7 miles to a junction with SR 169. Continue east on SE Kent Kangley Road for 3.4 miles and bear right onto Retreat Kanaskat Road SE. Now proceed for 3.1 miles and turn right onto Cumberland Kanaskat Road SE. Continue for 1.8 miles and turn right into Kanaskat-Palmer State Park and continue 0.9 mile to the day-use and picnic area.

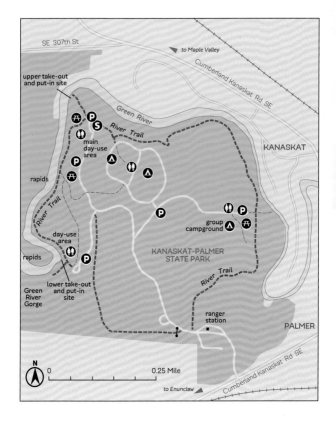

Named for two tiny communities on the Northern Pacific Railway in the heart of a once-thriving coal-mining district, Kanaskat-Palmer State Park is rife with history. But it's the Green River, which forms a big bend here at the mouth of a dramatic gorge, that is this park's main feature. While the park is well known for its river running, hikers will be pleased with the park's River Trail, which forms a pleasant kid-friendly 2.5-mile loop around the park. Aside from offering excellent views of the river, this trail leads to quiet riverside spots and traverses a few groves of big old trees too.

The author getting a close up look of the Green River

GET MOVING

River kayakers and rafters had been coming here long before it became a state park in 1983. It was some of these river rats who first recognized the ecological importance, natural beauty, and historical significance of the Green River Gorge and called for its preservation. In the 1970s, Washington State Parks began acquiring lands along the 12-mile stretch of the Green River Gorge for protection and recreation. Today a nearly contiguous stretch of protected land embraces the gorge from its mouth to its outlet.

Kanaskat-Palmer consists of 541-acres at the gorge's mouth. Here the river progresses from Class II to Class IV rapids, offering some of the most challenging river running on the Green River.

Starting from the main day-use area, locate the signed trailhead near the upper take-out and put-in site. Head east to begin hiking on a wide trail gently climbing to a junction in 0.1 mile. The spur right leads to the park's campground, with its forty-four wooded sites and six yurts. Head left along a bluff high above the river. Though much of the surrounding forest has been logged in the past, many mature trees can still be found along the way.

The forest floor is carpeted in ferns. In spring, wildflowers—particularly trilliums and bleeding hearts (*Dicentra*)—add dabs of white and purple to the emerald shroud.

The trail switchbacks off of the bluff, traversing a grove of big cottonwoods, hemlocks, spruces, and cedars and reaching river level and some good river views. Aside from looking for kayakers in the rapids, watch for mergansers and dippers in the frothy waters too. The trail now hugs the riverbank, coming to a junction at 0.8 mile. The spur right leads to the group campground. The spur left leads 0.1 mile to a deep pool graced with a sandy shore and a big cottonwood.

The River Trail continues straight through a lush alder flat before reaching a grove of big cedars. The way then bends right passing through a grove of Sitka spruce, a tree rare this far inland from the coast. Now on an old road bed, climb 100 feet up a bluff to arrive at the park road near the ranger station at 1.3 miles. Turn right and walk the road a short distance, picking up the trail again (signed) at a gate. Here, too, the way follows an old road bed, traversing a quiet forest away from the river.

Bear right at a junction. Eventually the roar of the river once again fills the forest as the trail reaches a bluff top above the waterway. Now slowly descend, reaching the park road once again at 1.9 miles. Turn left here and walk along the short road leading to the lower take-out and put-in site. Locate the River Trail once again and soon come to the lower take-out spot, located at a shaded cove at the mouth of the gorge.

Here the river cuts through 300-foot-tall bluffs and overhanging ledges of shale and sandstone. It is a very difficult place to explore—and you can catch glimpses of the deep gorge from various bridges and overlooks along the greenbelt protecting it. The River Trail heads upriver here, passing riverside ledges and boulders and roaring rapids. The river is lined with deciduous trees and hemlocks, giving this area a Southern Appalachian feel.

Continue upriver, passing excellent viewing spots. The trail eventually reaches the park picnic area, where a paved path right leads you back to your start. But before calling it a hike, be sure to walk the wide path left 0.1 mile to the upper take-out and put-in site for an excellent river view at a rocky bend.

36 **Nolte State Park**

DISTANCE:	1.5 miles of trails
ELEVATION GAIN:	Minimal
HIGH POINT:	800 feet
DIFFICULTY:	Easy
FITNESS:	Walkers, hikers, runners, bikers
FAMILY-FRIENDLY:	Yes
DOG-FRIENDLY:	On leash
AMENITIES:	Privies, water, picnic tables and shelters, benches, interpretive signs, playground, beach
CONTACT/MAP:	Washington State Parks
GPS:	N 47 16.203, W 121 56.469
BEFORE YOU GO:	Discover Pass required; park open 8:00 AM to dusk

GETTING THERE

Driving: From Tacoma, follow I-5 north to exit 142A and then follow State Route 18 east for 4.5 miles. Next take the exit for SR 164 (Auburn Way S) and turn left. Now follow SR 164 east for 7.1 miles and turn left onto SE 400th Street (Krain-Wabash Road) and drive for 6.9 miles. Then merge onto SE 392nd Street and continue 0.8 mile. Next turn left onto Veazie Cumberland Road SE and drive 1.5 miles. Turn left into Nolte State Park for parking and trailhead.

Once an old lake resort, now a delightful day-use state park, Nolte is mostly favored by visitors for its swimming, paddling, picnicking, and fishing. But it has a beautiful, wide easy-for-all trail that circles the park's main attraction—gorgeous big tree-lined Deep Lake. Languidly stroll around the lake looking for wildlife, or get your heart rate up and go for a run once or twice around it.

GET MOVING

While the old cabins (which once rented for $2.50 a night) have long been removed from the property, 117-acre Nolte State Park still retains the atmosphere of an old lake resort. In 1972, Minnie Nolte willed the family-owned resort to Washington State Parks. One of her stipulations was that the large Douglas firs on the property not be cut.

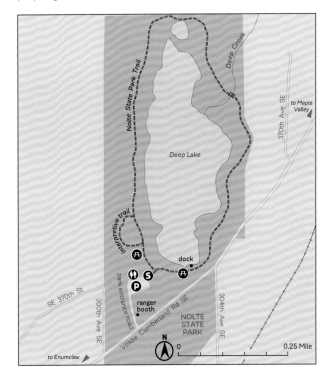

Stately firs at Nolte State Park

From the large parking lot (attesting to this park's popularity in the summer), locate the wide trail that circles the lake. If you follow it clockwise, you will soon come to a small interpretive trail that loops back to the main trail. The main trail heads along the lakeshore through beautiful groves of firs graced with an understory of vine maples, which add bright yellows to the deep emerald.

Though the lake is nearby, trees and shrubs obscure views of it. Several fishing paths branch off of the main trail, leading to favorite fishing holes and good lake views. The trail is graced with benches along the way and is nearly level in spots, but there are a few dips here and there. At the lake's northern end, the trail dips and skirts a marshy cove. Enjoy good views here across the lake.

Two more highlights along the trail are the bridged crossing of the lake's inlet stream and a huge overhanging alder. The trail then rounds the southern end of the lake, passing the fishing dock and traveling through a lakeside picnic area. Take a break here and enjoy the scene. Splashing, happy children add to this place's ambience as an accommodating summertime hangout. The lack of gas-powered boats on Deep Lake allows for some deep peace.

37 Pinnacle Peak

DISTANCE:	5 miles of trails
ELEVATION GAIN:	1000 feet
HIGH POINT:	1800 feet
DIFFICULTY:	Moderate to difficult
FITNESS:	Hikers
FAMILY-FRIENDLY:	Yes
DOG-FRIENDLY:	On leash
AMENITIES:	Privies, benches
CONTACT/MAP:	King County Parks
GPS:	N 47 10.704, W 121 58.411

GETTING THERE

Driving: Cal Magnusson (northern) Trailhead: From Tacoma, follow State Route 167 (River Road) east to Puyallup and continue on SR 167 (now the Valley Freeway) for 1.5 miles, taking the exit for SR 410. Follow SR 410 east for 14.8 miles and turn right onto SE 456th Street (before reaching the Enumclaw business district). Drive 1.2 miles east and turn right onto 276th Ave SE. Then continue 0.9 mile to the trailhead and parking on your right.

The southern trailhead: Follow SR 167 east to the exit for SR 410. Then continue east on SR 410 for 13.3 miles and turn right (just after crossing the White River) onto SE Mud Mountain Road. Next drive 1.8 miles to the parking lot and trailhead on your left.

From the north, it's a short but stiff little climb to this forested knob that rises abruptly out of the farmed flats south of Enumclaw. From the south, it's a little longer and a little gentler, but still a good workout to Pinnacle Peak's 1080-foot summit. An old fire-lookout site with a contested name, and nearly logged of its old growth in the 1980s, this little peak has a storied past. It has an interesting geological story to tell too—being the remnants of an old volcanic cone.

GET MOVING

A well-loved local hiking spot, little Pinnacle Peak almost got the axe. Back in 1979, while being managed by the Washington Department of Natural Resources, this timbered knoll was slated to be logged. But public opposition led to its being transferred to King County and eventually made into a park.

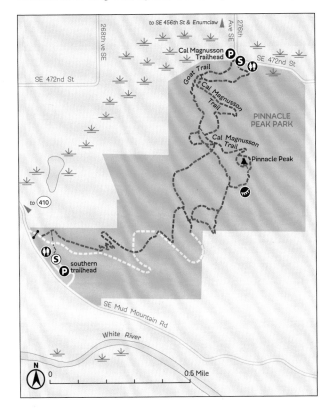

Pinnacle Peak rising above the Enumclaw countryside

Today the 375-acre Pinnacle Peak Park is one of the most popular hiking destinations in south King County.

You'll meet hikers of all ages, sizes, and abilities on this little peak. It's not uncommon, too, to see area workers getting in a quick trail run, aspiring climbers with heavy packs using this peak as a training ground, or groups of hikers on fitness challenges or treasure hunts. While this peak is popular, reaching the summit is not exactly a walk in the park. You'll gain 1000 feet of elevation in just one mile if you take the popular Cal Magnusson Trail. There are three other ways to the summit, with the easier approaches being from the southern trailhead.

From the Cal Magnusson Trailhead, follow the well-built and well-trodden trail upward! The Goat Trail, the old way to the summit, runs parallel with this trail. It's shorter, steeper, and the toughest way to the summit. A few spots on it make it not advisable for children. If you are thinking about doing a loop, it's best to go up the Goat and down the Cal Magnusson Trail.

The popular Magnusson Trail was named for a longtime mountaineer and REI employee. Young hikers will feel like they are traveling in this mountaineer's footsteps as they tackle this peak. While the trail's name is solid, this little mountain's name however is not so set. Long known by locals as Mount Pete and Mount Peak (which is redundant, no?), it eventually became Pinnacle Peak, named by King County Parks. You'll hear folks describing this little summit by all three of these names. And a popular peak in nearby Mount Rainier National Park named Pinnacle Peak can cause more confusion.

The way is shaded with big mature trees. A few breaks in the thick canopy offer window views to the farms and to Enumclaw below. You'll cross an old slide that can be slick. A cable here provides for some stability. Pass a couple of spurs to the Goat Trail too. At around 0.8 mile, the trail emerges on an old road. This is the old fire-tower access road and it makes for a longer and somewhat easier approach from the southern trailhead. From here, if you head right, it is about 1.5 miles to that trailhead. There are paralleling trails along this old road too, allowing for a loop variation if you choose to start your hike there—or do an up-and-over-and-back hike for a really good workout.

For the summit, continue left on the old road for 0.2 mile. Now gradually ascending, the way makes a switchback beneath a ledge of columnar basalt—further evidence of this peak's volcanic past. The road-trail then wraps around just beneath the summit to a view east over the White River Valley and to the Cascades foothills. A steep trail descends here to the south, and it can be followed a little over a tenth of a mile to a junction. Here you can hike right, following a trail about 0.2 mile through thick timber back to the old road. While this loop option is a little tough—it does lead past a view of Mount Rainier.

Of course, don't forget to take the short trail off of the old road to Pinnacle Peak's 1800-foot summit. It's anticlimactic with its old fire-lookout foundation blocks and no views to look out over. But you'll bag the summit, and that always feels like an accomplishment.

Next page: *Cottonwoods add golden touches to the trail come October.*

PUYALLUP

Named for the Puyallup tribe by Oregon Trail pioneer Ezra Meeker
(who became the city's first mayor), this city of 40,000, along with
nearby Orting (population 8000) and Sumner (population 10,000),
sits on the floodplain of the Puyallup River. In the shadow of Mount
Rainier, Puyallup and its neighbors once supported a large agricul-
tural economy (particularly daffodils). But housing developments
have replaced many of the area's farms within the last few decades,
despite the threat of future lahars and mudflows. The city contains
a viable downtown with several historic buildings and is known for
its antique shops and the Washington State Fair, one of the largest
fairs in the country. To Puyallup's immediate south is traffic-clogged,
unincorporated South Hill (population 60,000). The area's trail and
park system has been growing lately. It contains a couple of fine linear trails, including the long-distance Foothills Trail, which support-
ers hope will one day connect Tacoma to Mount Rainier.

38   Sumner Link Trail

DISTANCE:	5 miles one-way
ELEVATION GAIN:	Minimal
HIGH POINT:	70 feet
DIFFICULTY:	Easy
FITNESS:	Walkers, hikers, runners, bikers
FAMILY-FRIENDLY:	Yes, and jogger-stroller and wheelchair accessible
DOG-FRIENDLY:	On leash
AMENITIES:	Privies, benches, interpretive signs, exercise station
CONTACT/MAP:	City of Sumner Parks and Recreation
GPS:	N 47 14.147, W 122 14.196

GETTING THERE

Driving: From Tacoma, follow State Route 167 (River Road) east to Puyallup and continue on SR 167 (now the Valley Freeway) for 4 miles, taking the exit for 24th Street E. Then turn right and drive 0.6 mile to the trailhead at the road's end. Park on road shoulder.

Transit: Sound Transit lines 578 and 596 and the Sounder Lakewood light rail line stop in downtown Sumner near the trail.

Walk, run, or bike for more than 5 miles along the glacier-fed White River. Cross the river a couple of times and traverse pockets of riparian forest, a remnant daffodil farm, and the historic downtown of the little city of Sumner, named in honor of a Massachusetts senator and abolitionist who was caned in Congress by an opposing senator. When the weather is good, marvel at Mount Rainier hovering in the background. And when the "daffies" are blooming, prepare to be overwhelmed.

GET MOVING

Built to provide a link between the Lakeland Hills Trails, the Puyallup Riverwalk Trail (Trail 39), and eventually the Interurban Trail (Trail 25) and Foothills Trail (Trail 44), the Sumner

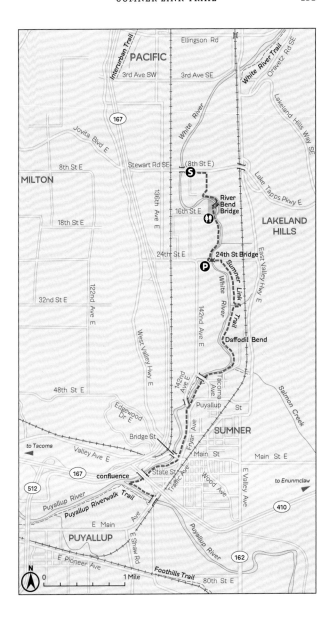

Link Trail is an excellent destination in its own right. This virtually level trail traverses the little city from north to south. While parts of it utilize sidewalks and involve several street crossings, the northern 2.5 miles is a sheer delight to run and walk. Here the trail follows alongside the river through farmland and a forested corridor—a remnant patch of what much of this valley between Puyallup and Renton looked like pre-Starbucks and Microsoft.

While you can access this trail from many points along the way, parking might be a challenge. The best place to park is along the cul-de-sac at the 24th Street E. Trailhead, near the north end of the trail. A full description of the trail from the north to south is provided here.

The trail begins from Stewart Road SE (8th Street E). There is no parking on this busy arterial. An attractive arch graces the start, along with milepost 0. The distance is marked along the way in half-mile increments. The trail travels south along

Explore the sights of the glacier-fed White River

a slough lined with tall cottonwoods. To the east is a defunct golf course (which, hopefully, could be saved for open space instead of more warehouses), while warehouses line the way west. The trail crosses the slough and meets up with the White River at a bend. The way then travels along the river and at 0.5 mile, crosses it on the River Bend Bridge, offering a gorgeous view of a slice of the pastoral valley just downriver.

The trail then passes a privy and spur leading to 16th Street E. and then continues south between river and slough. At 1.25 miles, after passing an exercise station, the way reaches the 24th Street Trailhead (parking available). Here it turns left to cross the river—then turns south again to travel along a remnant daffodil farm (now preserved and owned by the city). Views are excellent of glacial till bluffs to the east and Mount Rainier to the south. The trail makes a tight turn around a slough and once again hugs the river. Come to the Daffodil Bend interpretive area.

At 2.5 miles, warehouses and businesses start lining the east side of the trail. The river and a green swath lie to the west. At 2.8 miles, the trail parallels 149th Avenue SE. It then crosses Salmon Creek and comes to a junction. Here a short trail leads left—crossing the road and following along the creek. The Sumner Link Trail then pulls away from the road and passes more business—among them a coffee roaster, where the aroma will have you craving a cup o' joe.

At 3.2 miles, a spur leads left to Tacoma Avenue. Here you can walk a sidewalk on the Tacoma Avenue bridge and continue on an alternative 0.4-mile paralleling trail along the west side of the river. It meets back up with the main trail at 142nd Avenue E. The main trail ducks under Tacoma Avenue and reaches 142nd Avenue E. at 3.5 miles.

The trail then becomes a sidewalk (use caution at road crossings) along busy Fryar Avenue. At 4 miles, the way crosses Bridge Street at a busy intersection. It then continues right along Main Street, passing homes before resuming as a paved trail at 4.3 miles. The way then once again travels along the White River. It ducks under State Route 410 and skirts a sewage treatment plant. It then enters a greenbelt at the confluence of the White and Puyallup Rivers. A short spur leads right to the confluence. The Sumner Link Trail bends east and follows the Puyallup River upriver, coming to its end at E. Main Avenue (no parking) at 5 miles.

GO FARTHER

You can continue right on E. Main Avenue via sidewalks, cross the Puyallup River, and resume walking or running on the Puyallup Riverwalk Trail (Trail 39). At the Sumner Link Trail north end, though, it's best to wait until a safe link has been established before heading to the Lakeland Hills Trail in Auburn. The passage on foot currently involves lots of busy arterial crossings from the Sumner Link Trail. The paved 1.6-mile trail can safely be reached from Sunset Park on Lake Tapps Parkway E.

39　Puyallup Riverwalk Trail

DISTANCE:	4 miles one-way
ELEVATION GAIN:	Minimal
HIGH POINT:	50 feet
DIFFICULTY:	Easy
FITNESS:	Walkers, hikers, runners, bikers
FAMILY-FRIENDLY:	Yes, and jogger-stroller and wheelchair accessible
DOG-FRIENDLY:	On leash
AMENITIES:	Privies, benches
CONTACT/MAP:	City of Puyallup Parks and Recreation
GPS:	N 47 11.593, W 122 16.986
BEFORE YOU GO:	Open from half hour before sunrise to half hour after sunset; be aware that homeless camps are present along parts of this trail

GETTING THERE

Driving: From Tacoma, follow State Route 167 (River Road) east to Puyallup and turn right onto N. Meridian Avenue. After 0.2 mile, turn left onto 5th Avenue NE and drive 0.3 mile. Then turn right onto 5th Street NE and continue 0.2 mile. Next turn left onto 2nd Avenue NE and drive 0.2 mile to parking and trailhead on your left beneath the SR 512 bridge. Additional parking on the road.

Other Trail Access Points (all have parking): Veterans Park on 9th Avenue NE, Puyallup Skatepark on 4th Street NW, and just north of River Road on 11th Street NW.

Transit: Pierce Transit line 400 and Sound Transit line 578 stop at Puyallup Station a few blocks west of the trail. The Sounder Lakewood light rail line also stops at Puyallup Station.

Take a leisurely stroll or burn calories running on this paved path hugging the Puyallup River through the city. While the hustle and bustle of Puyallup are always nearby, the glacial river flowing from Mount Rainier will keep your attention. Towering cottonwoods provide plenty of shade along the way and in spring, cottony seeds fall upon the path like snow.

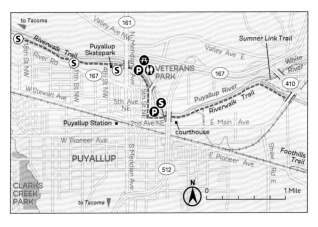

Savor the Riverwalk Trail as it meanders through Puyallup

GET MOVING

While the trail is officially 4 miles long, it actually consists of two sections: a 1.6-mile eastern stretch and a 1.8-mile western section, separated by a 0.6-mile section of sidewalk. The eastern portion is far more attractive, passing primarily through a greenbelt. The western portion travels close to shopping centers and busy roads and has a perennial problem with homeless encampments. The driving directions above are best for accessing the eastern half of the trail.

A description of the trail from west to east follows. The trail begins on River Road (SR 167) near 20th Street NW. From here it travels upriver, pretty close to the busy arterial. Traffic noise is a constant. The trail does dip below the levee in spots (flooding possible) and travels through a narrow green corridor. The river is always nearby and visible along this stretch. Despite the urban environment, look for eagles and wild critters.

The trail eventually pulls farther away from the road and comes to the 11st Street NW Trailhead at 0.6 mile. It then skirts behind businesses while still hugging the river. At 1.1 miles, it comes to the Skatepark Trailhead (parking available).

The trail then borders commercial centers before ducking under N. Meridian Avenue, skirting apartment complexes, and traveling through a stretch of big trees and manicured lawns. At 1.8 miles, the trail comes to Veterans Park (parking) complete with restrooms, a picnic shelter, and a beautiful wooden sculpture of a large snag with eagles.

From here the Riverwalk follows sidewalks south along 5th Street NE—then east on 2nd Avenue NE coming to the 2nd Avenue NE Trailhead (driving directions above) at 2.4 miles. The trail then resumes as an attractive paved path, ducking under the State Route 512 overpass. It then skirts a courthouse and hugs the river once more, entering a patch of forest dominated by towering cottonwoods. At 3 miles, it reaches a junction at a clearing. Here a soft-surface path travels south for 0.2 mile to E. Main Avenue near a bus stop (Pierce County line 409).

The Riverwalk Trail continues east through meadows and then back into forest buffered from busy city streets by a golf course. This section of trail is the most natural stretch of the Riverwalk and is quite attractive. The way continues through forest and grassy openings and then bends southeast where the White River flows into the Puyallup. The trail then hugs the river while skirting apartments, coming to its end at 4 miles at an Italian restaurant's parking lot (do not park here unless you're eating at the restaurant) on E. Main Avenue.

You may notice that the path continues under the E. Main Avenue bridge and adjacent railroad bridge, only to abruptly stop at a dirt farm road. Trail advocates are hoping to open a new stretch of trail here someday soon to connect with the nearby Foothills Trail (Trail 44).

GO FARTHER

Until the new section of trail is in place, if you want to keep going, cross the Puyallup River on the sidewalk on the E. Main Avenue bridge and then immediately pick up the Sumner Link Trail (Trail 38).

40 Wildwood Park

DISTANCE:	About 1.5 miles of trails
ELEVATION GAIN:	Up to 250 feet
HIGH POINT:	425 feet
DIFFICULTY:	Easy to moderate
FITNESS:	Walkers, runners
FAMILY-FRIENDLY:	Yes
DOG-FRIENDLY:	On leash
AMENITIES:	Exercise stations, picnic tables and shelters, privies, ball fields, playground
CONTACT/MAP:	City of Puyallup Parks and Recreation
GPS:	N 47 10.349, W 122 16.548
BEFORE YOU GO:	Open from 6:00 AM to half hour after sunset

GETTING THERE

Driving: From Tacoma, follow State Route 167 (River Road) to N. Meridian Avenue in Puyallup. Turn right and proceed 2 miles south. Then turn left onto 23rd Avenue SE and continue 0.6 mile. Turn left into Wildwood Park and then immediately turn right and proceed 0.2 mile to trailhead parking.

Transit: Pierce Transit line 425 stops on 7th Street SE near 23rd Avenue SE, from where it is a 0.25-mile walk to the park.

A heavily forested park on a hillside above the city, Wildwood Park is a popular place for a quick escape for a picnic or walk in the woods. The park is adorned, too, with historic artifacts from the 1930s. Challenge yourself on the park's exercise trail or just stroll on it, admiring the surrounding big trees and lush vegetation.

GET MOVING

Once owned by the local water company, Wildwood Park contains an old 1928-built reservoir. It also contains a manmade stone-lined waterfall that is quite pretty. During the 1930s, the

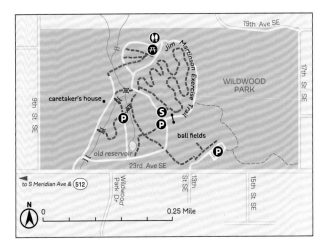

Works Progress Administration developed many of the facilities in the park, which still stand today and are appreciated for their simple rustic design.

The park contains 1.5 miles of trail or so, which thread the park's snaking narrow roads, small parking and picnic areas, and other features. Some of the park's roads are closed to vehicles, and they make good running and walking options as well. By combining roads and trails, you can get a decent little after-work walk or run in.

The park's main trail is the Jim Martinson Exercise Trail. It weaves for 0.7 mile through lush vegetation to a series of exercise stations. It makes for a good walk, too, if you're not interested in the stations. The trail crosses a couple of small creeks and includes a few little dips and upward grunts. There are some large mature cottonwoods and cedars along the way too.

The trail was named for local resident Jim Martinson, who lost both his legs in the Vietnam War and later became a gold medal athlete in both the summer and winter Paralympics, and won the wheelchair division in the 1981 Boston Marathon.

Jim Martinson Exercise Trail

In 2016 he was inducted into the US Ski and Snowboard Hall of Fame.

After you walk or run the Martinson Trail, walk or run the exterior roads in the park for a 0.9-mile loop that takes you through pretty forest, by the waterfall, and by the historic caretaker's home.

41 **Bradley Lake Park**

DISTANCE:	About 1.5 miles of trails
ELEVATION GAIN:	Minimal
HIGH POINT:	450 feet
DIFFICULTY:	Easy
FITNESS:	Walkers, runners
FAMILY-FRIENDLY:	Yes, and wheelchair accessible
DOG-FRIENDLY:	On leash
AMENITIES:	Picnic tables and shelter, restrooms, playground, ball fields
CONTACT/MAP:	City of Puyallup Parks and Recreation
GPS:	N 47 09.763, W 122 17.156
BEFORE YOU GO:	Open 6:00 AM to 8:00 PM, October 1 through March 31; and 6:00 AM to 10:00 PM, April 1 through September 30

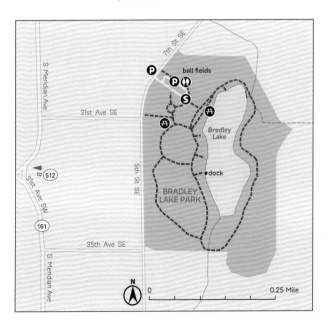

GETTING THERE

Driving: From Tacoma, follow I-5 south to exit 127 for State Route 512. Follow SR 512 east to Puyallup and take the exit for SR 161 south (31st Avenue SW). Go right on 31st Avenue SW and immediately turn left onto S. Meridian Avenue. Then in 0.1 mile, turn right onto 31st Avenue SE. Drive 0.2 mile and turn left onto 7th Street SE. Continue 0.1 mile and turn right into Bradley Lake Park for parking and trailhead. Overflow parking available across 7th Street SE from park entrance.

    Transit: Pierce Transit line 425 makes several stops west of the park.

Lovely little Bradley Lake sits just minutes from Puyallup's Meridian Avenue, clogged with traffic and sprawl. But here behind the sea of big box stores and strip malls is a 59-acre

Bradley Lake was once a peat bog

park graced with a 12-acre undeveloped lake, inviting lawns, and groves of towering mature conifers. A series of paved paths traverses the park and circles the lake to the delight of myriad folks of all ages and from all backgrounds.

GET MOVING

A former peat bog, Bradley Lake was formed in the 1980s after the owner of the property, Ward Bradley, dammed the bog's outlet upon ceasing peat mining. As the surrounding area succumbed to suburban sprawl, it's remarkable that the 59-acre tract encompassing the lake remained undeveloped. The City of Puyallup, through a bond, was able to purchase the property in 1997 and transform it into a top-notch park. Today Bradley Lake preserves a patch of greenery and a slice of the city's past and offers residents a great place to recreate together.

From the parking lot, follow a paved path down a rolling lawn toward the lake. Here you'll find picnic tables by the lakeshore—good places to sit with binoculars in hand to watch the resident birds. But you're here to walk or run, so that will have to wait. Follow the 0.8-mile loop path around the lake. It's a delightful trail that children will especially enjoy. The path cuts through open grassy areas along the lake's western shore and cool forest along its eastern reach. It's pretty level, with a few little pitches in the forested areas. You'll pass a dock where anglers are often perched. Juveniles under the age of fifteen, seniors, and disabled folks who possess a designated harvester companion card are allowed to drop a lure here.

While the loop trail is short, it's pretty and interesting enough to make multiple rounds on it—which many folks consistently do. But there are some other paths in the park too, including one that skirts around a meadow west of the lake and one that travels through an attractive forest in the park's southwest corner. And while Bradley Lake is pretty in rain or shine, when it's clear, expect to be wowed by views of Mount Rainier from along the lake's northern shoreline.

42 **Puyallup Loop Trail (Clarks Creek Park)**

DISTANCE:	More than 5 miles of trails
ELEVATION GAIN:	Up to 300 feet
HIGH POINT:	290 feet
DIFFICULTY:	Easy to moderate
FITNESS:	Walkers, hikers, runners
FAMILY-FRIENDLY:	Yes
DOG-FRIENDLY:	On leash
AMENITIES:	Picnic tables and shelter, restrooms, playground, ball fields and courts, off-leash dog park
CONTACT/MAPS:	Puyallup Parks and Recreation
GPS:	N 47 11.115, W 122 19.316
BEFORE YOU GO:	Park closes half hour after sunset

GETTING THERE

Driving:

From Puyallup, take the S. Meridian Avenue exit off of SR 512 and drive north 0.4 mile. Then turn left onto 7th Ave SW and continue for 1.3 miles. Then turn left into Clarks Creek Park for parking and trailhead.

From Tacoma, follow I-5 north and take exit 135 for E. 28th Street and State Route 167. At 0.2 mile, bear right onto Pioneer Way E. and follow for 5.2 miles. Then turn right onto S. Fruitland and continue for 0.2 mile. Next turn left onto 7th Ave SW. Drive 0.3 mile and turn right into Clarks Creek Park for parking and trailhead.

Transit: Pierce Transit line 409 stops on W. Pioneer Avenue and 18th Street SW. From here it is 0.5-mile walk south on 18th Street SW and west (right) on 7th Ave SW to the park.

Walk along a salmon-bearing creek or high above it at the edge of a steep ravine. Saunter through groves of towering evergreens and glades of verdant maples. And amble through

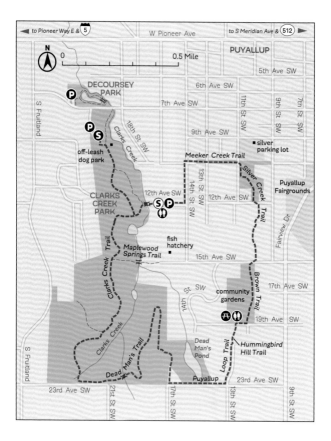

riparian forest on a lush floodplain. The Clarks Creek Park trail network takes you through a large greenbelt and quiet neighborhoods just a few minutes west of Puyallup's bustling downtown. Hike or run the whole Puyallup Loop in one big sweep, or just sample small sections one at a time.

GET MOVING

Puyallup's Clarks Creek Park has long contained a series of trails. But most of them were unmarked, poorly constructed user-built trails. A good and extended trail system here had long been on the city parks department's wish list. Finally in the summer of 2018, that dream came to fruition. The city acquired funding for new trail corridors and—with the help of the Washington Trails Association, parks officials, and volunteers—was able to upgrade and build new trails creating a large loop system. Many of the spur trails, however, are still poorly marked and built. Hopefully the parks department will be able to upgrade or close some of these user-built trails. In the meantime, take to the official Puyallup Loop Trail. It is well marked, and improvements are currently being made to it.

From the trailhead at Clarks Creek Park's north parking lot, follow the wide Clarks Creek Trail south, passing (or perhaps stopping at) the off-leash dog park. In 0.4 mile, the trail comes to a junction with the start of the Puyallup Loop at the south parking lot (restrooms and alternative south trailhead start, accessed from 12th Ave SW).

Utilizing the Clarks Creek Trail, the loop heads west, following an old road bed before bending left and climbing above the Clarks Creek floodplain. At 0.8 mile, reach a junction with the Maplewood Springs Trail. This spur trail drops down to Clarks Creek, crosses it on a bridge, and reaches the state fish hatchery on 15th Avenue SW in 0.25 mile.

The Clarks Creek Trail (loop) continues straight, steeply climbing at times and traversing steep slopes above the creek. The trail eventually reaches the creek's ravine rim and resumes a gentler grade. The surrounding forest is lush, thick, and full of vine maples and mature firs and big-leaf maples. You'll feel far removed from the city.

At 1.6 miles, the trail reaches 23rd Avenue SW, where it bends left across the head of the ravine and passes through an area being restored with native vegetation. The loop then follows the Dead Man's Trail, descending a bit to cross Clarks Creek (a trickle here), and passes big cedars and firs. The way then bends north and travels along the edge of the ravine

The author on the Puyallup Loop Trail

before reaching an old road and making a sharp turn right. It then gently climbs, passing some benches and reaching a small meadow graced with a native plant garden, and arrives at 23rd Avenue SW at 2.6 miles.

The trail now utilizes the shoulder of 23rd Avenue SW before turning left and following sidewalks north on 13th Street SW to reach the short Hummingbird Hill Trail. At 3.1 miles, it reaches 19th Avenue SW and follows it right for a short distance before resuming as the Brown Trail through the community gardens north of 19th Avenue SW (privy, picnic tables). It passes a big butternut tree and follows a grassy path to a creek, reaching 15th Avenue SW at 3.5 miles.

Then walk a short distance right on 15th Avenue SW and carefully cross it to pick up the Silver Creek Trail. The loop then skirts homes and fields at the edge of the Puyallup Fairgrounds and reaches 12th Avenue SW. It follows the road left and soon resumes as trail again on your right. The trail continues through riparian forest and floodplain, reaching 11th Street SW at 4 miles. The loop continues across the road on the·Meeker Creek Trail, which follows the creek and passes behind residences. It crosses 13th Street SW and continues on a dirt road, coming to 14th Street SW at 4.2 miles. The loop then heads left, following a sidewalk and road shoulder on 14th Street SW to 12th Avenue SW. Here it turns right, following a sidewalk back to Clarks Creek Park and reaching the south trailhead at 4.6 miles. The north trailhead can be reached by turning right and following the Clarks Creek Trail for 0.4 mile.

GO FARTHER

Check out adjacent DeCoursey Park to the north, where you can walk a delightful 0.3-mile loop around a small pond. It's short but very picturesque, and kids will love the piers and playground.

43   Nathan Chapman Memorial Trail

DISTANCE:	2.3 miles of trails
ELEVATION GAIN:	Minimal
HIGH POINT:	450 feet
DIFFICULTY:	Easy
FITNESS:	Walkers, runners, bikers
FAMILY-FRIENDLY:	Yes, and wheelchair accessible
DOG-FRIENDLY:	On leash
AMENITIES:	Picnic tables, restrooms, drinking water, playground, ball fields
CONTACT/MAP:	Pierce County Parks and Recreation
GPS:	N 47 07.663, W 122 18.845

GETTING THERE

Driving: From Tacoma, follow I-5 south to exit 127 for State Route 512. Follow SR 512 east to Puyallup and take the exit for 94th Avenue E. Then drive south on 94th Avenue E. for 1.3 miles. Next turn right onto 128th Street E and continue for 0.5 mile. Then

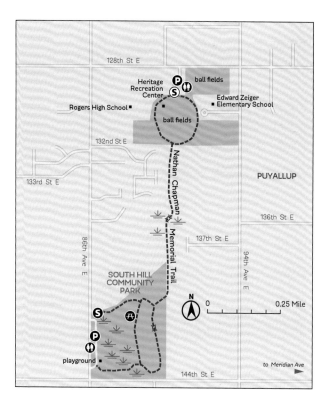

turn left onto 86th Avenue E. and drive 0.8 mile. Then turn left into the South Hill Community Park for trailhead and parking.

Walk or run on this peaceful path winding through wetlands and groves of towering timber. Paved and nearly level, the Nathan Chapman Memorial Trail is ideal for folks of all ages and abilities. If you connect South Hill Community Park and its loop trail with the Heritage Recreation Center and its loop trail, you can get a decent little walk or run in here. Utilizing curving bridges and boardwalks, and lined with split-rail fencing in spots, this trail is well designed and aesthetically appealing.

Open forest and pocket meadows along the trail

GET MOVING

There are several interconnecting paths within the South Hill Community Park and a connector path to the Heritage Recreation Center, collectively referred to as the Nathan Chapman Memorial Trail. Army Sergeant First Class Nathan Chapman was a South Hill resident and a Green Beret, who, in 2002, became the first American to die by enemy fire in Afghanistan. A veteran of combat and a decorated soldier, Chapman served in the armed forces for more than twelve years. He died at age thirty-one, leaving behind a wife and two children. The trail was dedicated in 2005.

From the trailhead, you can head off straight into the woods, crossing a creek and coming to a junction in 0.2 mile. Here you can head right and loop 0.6 mile back to your start. Another trail branches from that trail, which allows you to loop back to this junction in 0.4 mile. Both options are good for a short walk or as a nice add-on to the longer option of going all the way to the Heritage Recreation Center. The shorter loop options include a fenced route through a mixed forest of coniferous and deciduous trees including Oregon ashes, trees that are pushing their northern limits here.

The main trail reaches the second loop option junction 0.1 mile beyond the first junction. If you head right at the second junction, you'll circle around open meadows and the park's playground. If you head left at the second junction, you'll travel through attractive forest and cross a small stream.

The northern route traverses a forest sporting mature firs and crosses, via boardwalks and bridges, a large wetland area flush with bulrushes and a bevy of birdlife. The abundance of cottonwoods, willows, maple, ash, and cascara add golden hues to this trail in autumn, making it exceptionally delightful.

The nearly level trail then cuts across a powerline swath and skirts a wetland area and small pond—yet another spot to stop and watch for wildlife. At 0.6 mile from the second junction (0.9 mile from the trailhead) the trail terminates at the Heritage Recreation Center (alternative parking and start) with its many ball fields and soccer fields. If games aren't in session and the area is pretty quiet, consider continuing your walk or run on the Heritage Center's 0.5-mile trail that loops around the baseball fields. The loop is lined with red maples (an Eastern US native) whose foliage turns fiery red in the fall, making this loop quite dynamic for a few weeks each year.

44 Foothills Trail

DISTANCE:	21 miles one-way
ELEVATION GAIN:	Up to 650 feet
HIGH POINT:	725 feet
DIFFICULTY:	Easy
FITNESS:	Walkers, runners, bikers
FAMILY-FRIENDLY:	Yes, and the paved trail is jogger-stroller and wheelchair accessible
DOG-FRIENDLY:	On leash
AMENITIES:	Restrooms, benches
CONTACT/MAP:	Pierce County Parks and Recreation
GPS:	N 47 11.047, W 122 14.708

GETTING THERE
Driving:

East Puyallup Trailhead: From Tacoma, follow State Route 167 (River Road) east to Puyallup and turn right onto N. Meridian Ave. After 0.6 mile, turn left onto E. Pioneer Ave. Drive 2.1 miles and turn left onto 134th Avenue E, cross the trail, and immediately turn right onto 80th Street E. Then drive 0.3 mile to trailhead on your right.

Buckley Trailhead: From Tacoma, follow SR 167 (River Road) east to Puyallup and continue on SR 167 (now the Valley Freeway) for 1.5 miles, taking the exit for State Route 410. Drive east on SR 410 for 11.8 miles to junction with State Route 165 in Buckley. Turn right on SR 165 and immediately come to the trailhead on your right.

Other Trail Access Points (all have parking and privies): McMillin Trailhead on State Route 162 and 140th Street E., between Sumner and Orting; Orting Trailhead in Central Park, near the junction with Washington Avenue S. (SR 162) and Calistoga Street W.; and South Prairie Trailhead, located off of SR 162 (Pioneer Way E), near the junction with Emery Avenue S.

One of the finest and most scenic rail trails in the Puget Sound region, the Foothills National Recreation Trail travels for 21 paved miles from farms in the Puyallup River Valley to forested hills and the White River in Buckley. The route travels along glacier-fed waterways. And majestic glacier-covered Mount Rainier can be seen hovering above the countryside from many points along the way. The trail travels over restored trestle bridges, across farmland, and through two quaint small-city downtowns. Run, walk, or bike the entire trail in one glorious sweep, or savor sections of it on multiple trips.

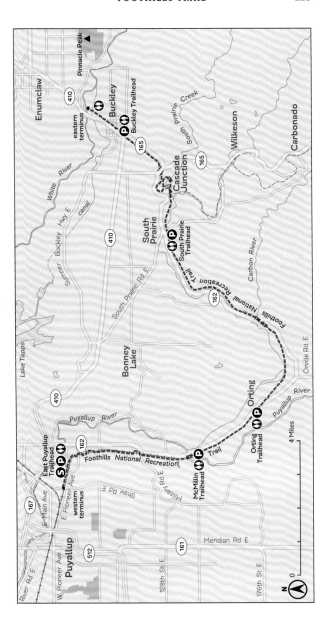

GET MOVING

The Foothills Trail has been a work in progress since 1990; government and citizen visionaries and a slew of dedicated volunteers have helped make the trail a reality and the pride of the communities it runs through. The Foothills Trail utilizes a former rail line that once ran from Tacoma to Ellensburg. The western terminus of the trail is actually a half mile west of the East Puyallup Trailhead. Below is a brief description of the trail from west to east.

The trail starts along E. Pioneer Avenue (no parking) at the junction with Shaw Road E. It then passes through the East Puyallup Trailhead and skirts rural residences, crossing E. Pioneer Avenue at 1 mile. It then cuts through farmland, crosses N. 96th Street East at 1.8 miles, travels across more farms,

Carbon River east of Orting

and crosses Military Road E. at 3.2 miles. Along the way, the trail parallels active railroad tracks. Be sure to use caution at all railroad and road crossings. The way now parallels SR 162, traversing countryside that begins to transition into suburban housing developments. At 4.8 miles, just after crossing the Puyallup River on the first of several restored trestle bridges, the trail reaches the McMillin Trailhead. This trailhead, like the East Puyallup and South Prairie Trailheads, are designed to look like miniature train depots.

The trail soon enters Orting city limits and passes several tract housing developments. The way is lined with various ornamental trees that produce pretty blossoms in the spring. Mount Rainier creates a stunning backdrop. Closer to the city's center, the trail skirts several restaurants that may entice you to take a break. At 7.6 miles, it reaches Orting's pretty Central Park with its daffodil-themed bell tower.

The trail continues east, crosses SR 162, and leaves the city, reaching the banks of the Carbon River at 8.4 miles. The next section is among the prettiest, with close-up views of the roiling glacier-fed river and eight bridges, including several restored trestles. There are also a handful of rest stops and benches along this stretch. The trail comes upon SR 162 again—and runs parallel to the highway and the Carbon River—then crosses the highway on a bridge at 10.3 miles. A quarter mile farther, it crosses the Carbon River on a trestle.

The way then cuts through a forested corridor before paralleling South Prairie Creek. Continuing through a pastoral countryside, the trail leaves the creek at 12.6 miles. It then runs between SR 162 and the South Prairie Carbon River Road, reaching the South Prairie Trailhead in the tiny community of South Prairie at 15.2 miles.

At 15.5 miles, the trail crosses South Prairie Creek again, then traverses an RV park before reaching Cascade Junction at 16.2 miles. Here an unimproved section of rail trail continues south to Carbonado (see Go Farther). The Foothills Trail continues left, crossing South Prairie Creek once more and skirting a large wetland. At 17 miles, the trail crosses Lower Burnett Road E. It then begins climbing out of a ravine to a plateau via a sweeping, looping switchback.

The way skirts country homes and travels up a small ravine, darting under a high bridge (SR 162) at 18.3 miles. It then bends northeast and, paralleling SR 165, makes a linear approach to Buckley. At 19.6 miles, it reaches the Buckley Trailhead at the junctions of SR 165 and SR 410. The trail then continues another 1.4 miles through little Buckley, traversing park lawns and the downtown business district. A few restaurants and cafés call out for you to take a break. At 21 miles, the trail comes to its current end at the White River.

GO FARTHER

Funding has been approved, and by 2021 a new bridge will span the White River, extending the Foothills Trail all the way to Enumclaw. You can currently walk, run, or bike Enumclaw's 2.3-mile section of trail by accessing a trailhead on SE 456th Street just east of SR 410.

From Cascade Junction, an unimproved soft-surface section of old railroad bed continues all the way to the old coal-mining towns of Burnett, Wilkeson, and Carbonado. Unfortunately the trail crosses private property shortly past Cascade Junction, prohibiting you from exploring this section from this direction. You can, however, park near the Wilkeson Fire Department and access the trail from there. After a short paved section, you can walk, run, or mountain bike along the trail for 3 miles south to Carbonado or 2.5 miles north to a trestle. Trail officials and the Foothills Rails-to-Trails Coalition are working hard to improve this section of trail and connect it to the existing section. They are also working on connecting the trail to the Puyallup Riverwalk Trail (see Trail 39).

ACKNOWLEDGMENTS

AS WITH ALL OF MY previous books, researching and writing *Urban Trails: Tacoma* was fun, gratifying, and a lot of hard work. I couldn't have finished this project without the help and support of the following people. A huge thank you to all the great people at Mountaineers Books; especially publisher, Helen Cherullo, editor-in-chief, Kate Rogers, and project manager Emily White.

A big thank you to my editor Erin Cusick for her attention to detail and thoughtful suggestions helping to make this book a finer volume. I also want to thank my wife, Heather, and son, Giovanni, for accompanying me on many of the trails in this book. A big thanks too to Virginia Scott for tagging along on several of the trails. And I thank God for watching over me and keeping me safe and healthy while I hiked, biked, and ran all over Tacoma!

RESOURCES

CONTACTS AND MAPS

Anderson Island Parks and Recreation District
http://andersonislandparks.org/

City of Auburn
253-931-3043 | www.auburnwa.gov/things_to_do/parks_trails

City of Black Diamond
360-886-5700 | www.ci.blackdiamond.wa.us/Depts/NaturalResources/parks
.html

City of DuPont
253-912-5245 | www.ci.dupont.wa.us/index.aspx?nid=187

City of Federal Way
253-835-6911 | www.cityoffederalway.com/parks

City of Lakewood
253-983-7887 | www.cityoflakewood.us/parks-and-recreation/parks

City of Maple Valley
425-432-9953 | www.maplevalleywa.gov/departments-services
/parks-recreation/parks-and-trails

City of Milton
253-922-8733 | www.cityofmilton.net/general-information/parks-trails

City of Puyallup
253-841-5457 | www.cityofpuyallup.org/250/City-of-Puyallup-Parks

Town of Steilacoom
253-581-1912 | www.townofsteilacoom.com/165/Parks

City of Sumner
253-299-5714 | https://sumnerwa.gov/living/recreation/trails

City of Tacoma
253-305-1030 | www.metroparkstacoma.org

Green River College Trails
www.instruction.greenriver.edu/naturalresources/images/GRCCtrailmap5.jpg

King County Metro Transit
https://kingcounty.gov/depts/transportation/metro

King County Parks
www.kingcounty.gov/services/parks-recreation/parks
/parks-and-natural-lands/parksatoz

Pierce County Ferry (from Steilacoom to Anderson Island)
www.co.pierce.wa.us/1793/Ferry

Pierce County Parks and Recreation
www.piercecountywa.org/114/Parks-Recreation

Pierce Transit
www.piercetransit.org

Scott Pierson Trail
www.piercecountywa.org/DocumentCenter/View/24383

Sound Transit
www.soundtransit.org

Washington State Parks
360-902-8844 | https://parks.state.wa.us

TRAIL AND CONSERVATION ORGANIZATIONS

Earth Corps
www.earthcorps.org/our-story/hylebos/

Foothills Rails-to-Trails Coalition
www.piercecountytrails.org

Forterra
http://forterra.org

Friends of Cedar Creek Park
www.friendsofcedarcreekpark.org

Greater Metro Parks Foundation
www.metroparksfoundation.org

King County Parks Foundation
https://kingcountyparksfoundation.org

The Mountaineers
www.mountaineers.org

Nature Conservancy
www.nature.org

Tahoma Audubon Society
www.tahomaaudubon.org

Washington State Parks Foundation
https://waparks.org

Washington Trails Association
www.wta.org

Washington Wildlife and Recreation Coalition
www.wildliferecreation.org

RUNNING AND HIKING CLUBS AND ORGANIZED EVENTS

Bear Run
This long-running 5K run and walk is held at Lake Wilderness Park and utilizes
area trails, including the Green to Cedar Rivers Trail.
www.maplevalleybearrun.com

Defiance 50K
Ultra-run trail races include a 50K, 30K, and 15K, and take place at Point Defiance Park.
http://defiance50k.com

Evergreen Trail Runs
Annual trail-running races are held at various Eastside and South Sound Parks,
including Dash Point State Park.
www.evergreentrailruns.com

Lake Wilderness Run
This multisport event is staged from Maple Valley's Lake Wilderness Park. The
5.5K and 10K utilize the Green to Cedar Rivers Trail, and the half marathon
utilizes both the Green to Cedar Rivers Trail and the Cedar River Trail.
http://lakewildernessrun.com

The Mountaineers
The Seattle-based outdoors club has a Tacoma Branch (and clubhouse located
in Old Town) that is involved with local conservation issues as well as coordinat-
ing group outdoor activities.
www.mountaineers.org/locations-lodges/tacoma-branch/about

Orting Turkey Trot
Races include a 5K, 10K, and half marathon on the Foothills Trail.
www.databarevents.com/ortingturkeytrot

Rainer to Ruston Relay
This fifty-mile relay is held on the Foothills Trail (to raise funds for the trail), Puyallup Riverfront Trail, and Ruston Way Path.
www.rainiertoruston.com

Run Lakewood
A series of organized races of various distances, with several held at Fort Steilacoom Park.
https://runlakewood.com

St. Paddy's Day Run Tacoma
St. Patrick's Day themed races—5K, 10K, half marathon and relay—are held on the Ruston Way Path and Waterwalk.
www.stpaddyruntacoma.com

Swan Creek 5K
This family-friendly race is sponsored by Tacoma Metro Parks and held at Swan Creek Park.
www.metroparkstacoma.org/races

Tacoma Narrows Half Marathon
This large race utilizes the Scott Pierson Trail on the Tacoma Narrows Bridge.
http://tacomanarrowshalf.com

Woof Woof Walk
An organized 1.5-mile and 3-mile costume walk for both two- and four-legged participants, the Woof Woof Walk is held near Halloween at Spanaway Park.
www.co.pierce.wa.us/1279/Woof-Woof-Walk

INDEX

ABOUT THE AUTHOR

Heather, Giovanni, and Craig

CRAIG ROMANO grew up in rural New Hampshire, where he fell in love with the natural world. He moved to Washington in 1989 and has since hiked more than 25,000 miles in the Evergreen State. An avid runner as well, Craig has run more than one hundred half marathons and twenty-five marathons and ultra runs, including the Boston Marathon, Rainier to Ruston 50K, and the White River 50 Mile Endurance Run.

Craig is an award-winning author of more than twenty books; his *Columbia Highlands: Exploring Washington's Last Frontier* was recognized in 2010 by Washington Secretary of State Sam Reed and State Librarian Jan Walsh as a "Washington Reads" book for its contribution to Washington's cultural heritage. Craig also writes for numerous publications, tourism websites, and http://hikeoftheweek.com.

When not hiking, running, and writing, he can be found napping with his wife, Heather; son, Giovanni; and cat, Giuseppe, at his home in Skagit County. Visit him online at www.Craig Romano.com and on Facebook at Craig Romano Guidebook Author.

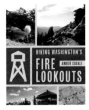
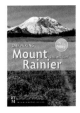